Easy Ways to
ENLARGE YOUR GERMAN VOCABULARY

Karl A. Schmidt

DEPARTMENT OF MODERN LANGUAGES,
UNIVERSITY OF SAN FRANCISCO

DOVER PUBLICATIONS, INC.
NEW YORK

Published in Canada by General Publishing
Company, Ltd., 30 Lesmill Road, Don Mills,
Toronto, Ontario.
Published in the United Kingdom by Constable
and Company, Ltd.

*Easy Ways to Enlarge Your German Vocabu-
lary* is a new work, first published by Dover Publications, Inc., in 1974.

International Standard Book Number:
0-486-23044-9
Library of Congress Catalog Card Number:
73-92020

Manufactured in the United States of America
Dover Publications, Inc.
180 Varick Street
New York, N.Y. 10014

PREFACE

This text attempts to work on a systematic build-up of German vocabulary
through the understanding of German prefixes, suffixes and other word-
building devices. It is somewhat surprising to see how greatly this
subject has been neglected in German language books while grammatical
and phonological features have always received full attention. At the
most, vocabulary discussion is introduced piecemeal in widely scattered
paragraphs. The present work is the first attempt in many years to tackle
the crucial vocabulary question vigorously and systematically.

The book is designed for use at the intermediate level. The first section,
dealing with the study of the etymological relationship between English
and German, can be used as early as the second college semester. It is
understood that the material in this volume will serve, along with a
regular language text, as an additional aid for word study.

Extensive practice exercises should improve the student's insight into
the nature of word formation and help to gain command of a sizeable
German vocabulary. Almost each principle of derivation is followed by
one or more exercises which the student will work out for himself. A
Key to all suggested exercises allows him to verify the exact form and
meaning of the derivative in question.

Special attention has been given to the use and analysis of verbal prefixes
and the manner in which these can modify the meaning of root words. However,
there was no intention of exhausting the subject of word formation.

CONTENTS

A. LINGUISTIC RELATIONSHIP BETWEEN GERMAN AND ENGLISH

The following study is intended to offer an insight into the relationship of German and English vocabulary. A thorough understanding of the nature of this kinship will improve considerably the student's ability to read and pick up a sizeable German vocabulary.

German and English are both members of the Germanic branch of the Indo-European family of languages. Words of Germanic origin, i.e. in English those derived from Anglo-Saxon, make up the most basic and essential segment of the vocabulary of the two languages. For example, the sentence :

> "I am hungry, thirsty, weary, cold and naked; give me food, drink, a bed, fire and clothing"

is of purely Anglo-Saxon origin, and the similarity of these words with their German counterparts is evident.

Such words, which have the same root in the parent language, are called cognates. Hundreds of these cognates look so much alike that they need no further explanation.

I. FULL COGNATES

Finger	finger	Wolf	wolf
Hand	hand	Hammer	hammer
Arm	arm	Sack	sack
Lippe	lip	Wanderer	wanderer
Nest	nest	Winter	winter
Ring	ring	Hunger	hunger
Rose	rose	Gold	gold
warm	warm	Land	land
mild	mild	Plan	plan
bitter	bitter	finden *)	find
so	so	binden *)	bind

However, the majority of cognates are not so clearly identifiable as those listed above simply because their similarity has been obscured by the so-called "sound shift" or LAUTVERSCHIEBUNG. The great German philologist Jakob Grimm, more popularly known as a collector of fairy tales, was the first one to observe and describe a pattern of consonant changes or sound shifts within the Germanic language family. This phenomenon, often referred to as Grimm's Law, was instrumental in producing the difference between Low German (e.g. Anglo-Saxon) and High German. Thus many German words which a student of German will come to know will really be English words in disguise. We will, therefore, summarize those relationships between the two languages, which seem most important from the standpoint of better understanding German vocabulary.

---

*) Drop the German infinitive ending -en in order to get the stem of the verb.

II. PARTIAL COGNATES

1. Consonant Relationship

GERMAN		ENGLISH	
b	:	b (initial)	Bett (bed), haben (have), Leber (liver)
		v (medial)	Silber (silver), Rabe (raven), sieben (seven)
		f (final)	**Weib (wife)**, Kalb (calf), halb (half)
ch	:	k	Buch (book), Kuchen (cake), Milch (milk), Mönch (monk), machen (make), Storch (stork)
cht	:	ght	recht (right), Sicht (sight), Nacht (night), brachte (brought), Macht (might), Licht (light)
d	:	th	Bad (bath), Ding (thing), dick (thick), dies (this), danken (thank), Dieb (thief)
f	:	f (initial)	Feuer (fire), helfen (help), offen (open)
		p (medial, final)	Affe (ape), hoffen (hope), reif (ripe)
g	:	y	Garn (yarn), gestern (yesterday), sagen (say), legen (lay), Tag (day), Weg (way)
k	:	ch or c	Kirche (church), Kammer (chamber), Käse (cheese), Kinn (chin), kühl (cool), Kultur (culture), Kur (cure), Küfer (cooper)
mm	:	mb (silent b)	Lamm (lamb), dumm (dumb), Kamm (comb), Nummer (number)
n (retained)	:	n (dropped)	Gans (goose), fünf (five), Stern (star), Wunsch (wish)
pf	:	p or pp	Pfund (pound), Pfanne (pan), Pfeife (pipe), Pfad (path), Apfel (apple), Kupfer (copper)
s,ss z,tz	:	t *)	das (that), Wasser (water), Fuss (foot), heiss (hot), zwei (two), setzen (set), Hass (hate), sitzen (sit), Herz (heart), zehn (ten), Witz (wit)
sch	:	sh (before vowels)	scheu (shy), scharf (sharp), Schiff (ship), Schuh (shoe), scheinen (shine), Fisch (fish)
	:	s (before consonants)	Schmied (smith), Schmutz (smut), Schwalbe (swallow), Schwein (swine), schmieren (smear)
t	:	d	Gott (God), gut (good), selten (seldom), tief (deep), Tod (death), Seite (side), gleiten (glide)

*) The German <u>t</u> in combinations like <u>cht</u> and <u>st</u> is protected by preceding consonants, and does not shift to <u>s</u> or <u>z</u> :

Sicht	(sight)		Stein	(stone)
recht	(right)		Strasse	(street)

2. Vowel Relationship

GERMAN		ENGLISH	
a	:	o	alt (old), lang (long), Nase (nose), Kamm (comb)
a	:	ea	klar (clear), Jahr (year), Bart (beard), nah (near)
au	:	ou	Haus (house), Maus (mouse), sauer (sour), aus (out)
e	:	i	leben (live), geben (give), recht (right), Schwester (sister)
ei	:	i	beissen (bite), Meile (mile), mein (mine), Wein (wine)
ei	:	o	beide (both), Heim (home), Stein (stone), meist (most)
ei	:	ea	heilen (heal), Heide (heath), reichen (reach), Schweiss (sweat)
ie	:	ee	Bier (beer), Knie (knee), fliehen (flee), Tier (deer)
o	:	u	Sonne (sun), Sommer (summer), Onkel (uncle), Donner (thunder)
o	:	ea	Strom (stream), Bohne (bean), Ohr (ear), Ost (east)
u	:	oo	Buch (book), Fuss (foot), Schule (school), Futter (food)
u	:	ou	rund (round), jung (young), Suppe (soup), Gruppe (group)

III. COGNATES DIFFERING IN MEANING

In deriving the meaning of German words from English cognates the student should note that there are a number of words which, though very similar in form, may have different meanings in the two languages. The following are some familiar examples:

German	English Meaning	English Cognate
das Bein	leg	bone
die Blume	flower	bloom
eitel	vain	idle
handeln	to act	handle
die Hose	trousers	hose
der Knabe	boy	knave
der Tisch	table	dish
weil	because	while
streng	strict, severe	strong
sterben	to die	starve
Knecht	servant, farm-hand	knight
Baum	tree	beam
schlimm	bad	slim

NOTE: If the English cognate does not make sense use the context or a dictionary to determine the meaning of the German word.

- 3 -

Practice 1 :

With the help of the clues provided, guess the meanings of the following words, dropping the German endings and prefixes that are underlined.

reiten	tief	treiben	Tat	rot	laut	Teufel
waten	falten	Blut	Not	Karte	teuer	Wort
Dorn	Norden	Erde	Feder	Denker	Distel	Durst
Donner	dünn	drei	dein			
Zinn	erzählen	begrüssen	besser	Katze	Zoll	Pflanze
Zweig	Zunge	Netz	Salz	Hitze	Sitz	zwanzig
Pfeffer	Pfosten	Pfennig	Seife	Waffe	Schaf	auf
laufen	Harfe	Bischof		Schiff	schlafen	
streben	Sieb	**Rabe**	weben	heben	eben	haben
brechen	sprechen	Rechen	wachen	Woche	Joch	Becher
Gewicht	Gefecht	Fracht	leicht	dachte	mochte	acht

Practice 2 :

Give the English equivalent for the following sentences:

1. Der Steward bringt Kaffee, Tee und eine kalte Platte mit Brot, Butter und Käse. 2. Die Disteln auf der Heide haben scharfe Dornen. 3. Die Katze sitzt auf dem Feld; sie ist hungrig und will eine Maus. 4. Sie brachten acht Lichter ins Haus und wachten bis Mitternacht. 5. Maria hat blondes Haar, blaue Augen und eine lange Nase. 6. Im Sommer können sie in den Alpen wandern, fischen, schwimmen und segeln. 7. Die meisten Touristen fahren ins Ausland und schreiben Postkarten an ihre Familien. 8. Der Passagier starrt auf das Wasser des Ozeans. Was sieht er im Wasser ? Es ist ein Eisberg. 9. Wenn alles gut geht, landen wir in zehn Minuten in Frankfurt. 10. Der Koch bäckt Apfelkuchen und kocht Fleischsuppe. 11. Wenn es kühl ist, reitet er nicht ins Tal. 12. Der alte Vater hat zwei Söhne und eine Tochter.

IV. WORDS OF FOREIGN ORIGIN

Many words of Latin and Greek origin, the most general terms of the arts
and sciences, are part of the international language bank, and therefore
are likewise shared by both German and English. It takes little imagination
to discover the close similarities between these international terms in
both languages. The few slight deviations, noticeable mainly in the
suffixes or endings, will be shown in the table below. Remember that English
c usually changes to k or z in German. There is also a difference in the
word accent: German words of foreign origin are stressed on the final
syllable or next to it.

1. Nouns

Noun suffixes, whether of German or non-German origin, always determine the
gender and the plural form of the derivative; e.g. the word "Nation" like
all other nouns ending in -ion, is feminine and forms the plural in -en.

a. Masculine Nouns

German	English	Change
der Direktor, -en	director	-
der Lektor, -en	lector	-
der Konsonant, -en	consonant	-
der Protestant, -en	protestant	-
der Korrespondent, -en	correspondent	-
der Student, -en	student	-
der Monarchismus	monarchism	-ismus = ism
der Marxismus	Marxism	

Agent nouns *)can be derived from such nouns by changing -ismus to -ist.

German	English	Change
der Monarchist, -en	monarchist	-
der Marxist, -en	Marxist	-
der Techniker, -	technician	-iker = -ician
der Mechaniker, -	mechanic	-ker = -ic

b. Feminine Nouns

All with plural in -(e)n

German	English	Change
die Promenade, -n	promenade	-
die Parade, -n	parade	-
die Passage, -n	passage	-
die Massage, -n	massage	-
die Nation, -en	nation	-
die Position, -en	position	-

*)Agent nouns designate persons who are active in a particular field or science
(often a profession).

die Substanz, -en	substance	-anz = -ance
die Dissonanz, -en	dissonance	
die Tendenz, -en	tendency	-enz = -ence/ency
die Korrespondenz, -en	correspondence	
die Monarchie, -n	monarchy	-ie = -y
die Psychologie	psychology	
die Mechanik	mechanics	-ik = -ic(s)
die Republik, -en	republic	
die Stabilität	stability	-ität= -ity
die Brutalität, -en	brutality	
die Hypnose, -n	hypnosis	-ose = -osis
die Tuberkulose	tuberculosis	
die Literatur, -en	literature	-ur = -ure
die Architektur, -en	architecture	

c. Neuter Nouns

The remaining cognate nouns of non-German origin are mostly neuter. However, there is a small number of suffixes with varying gender, i.e. neuter or masculine.

das Konsulat, -e	consulate	-at = -at(e)
das Sekretariat, -e	secretariat(e)	
das Album, die Alben	album	-
das Aquarium, die Aquarien	aquarium	-
das Vokabular, -e	vocabulary	-ar/är = ary
das Militär	military	
der Funktionär, -e	functionary	
der Notar, -e	notary	
das Papier, -e	paper	-ier = -er
das Quartier, -e	quarters	-ier = -ers
das Brevier, -e	breviary	-ier = -iary
der Bankier, -e	banker	-ier = -er

Some neuter cognates with plural in -s :

das Radio, -s, das Cafe, -s, das Hotel, -s, das Motel, -s, das Casino, -s, das Milieu, -s, das Restaurant, -s, das Hobby, -s, das Radar, -s, das Sofa, -s, das Porto, -s.

2. Adjectives

German	English	Change
zentral	central	-
pastoral	pastoral	
intelligent	intelligent	-
prominent	prominent	
sensationell	sensational	-ell = -al
traditionell	**traditional**	
realistisch	realistic	-isch = -ic(al)
klinisch	clinical	
attraktiv	attractive	-iv = -ive
impulsiv	impulsive	
skandalös	scandalous	-ös = -ous
religiös	religious	

3. Verbs

The infinitive ending -ieren is the only foreign suffix that is used in
German. Its first syllable always carries the word stress. Remember that
the past participle does not have a ge- prefix (er hat studiert).

German	English	Change
passieren	to pass	
existieren	to exist	
diktieren	to dictate	-ieren = -ate
dividieren	to divide	-ieren = -e
definieren	to define	
mobilisieren	to mobilize	**-isieren = -ize**
sozialisieren	to socialize	
identifizieren	to identify	**-fizieren = -fy**
klassifizieren	to classify	

Practice 3 :

In accordance with the model, form the agent-nouns and the adjectives from
the words provided. Watch the word accent indicated on the model.

Model: der Kapitalísmus   der Kapitalíst   kapitalístisch
       der Idealísmus   der Idealíst   idealístisch

(Abstract Noun)	(Agent Noun)	(Adjective)
-ismus	-ist	-istisch

der Militarismus
der Sozialismus
der Positivismus
der Nihilismus
der Tourismus
der Separatismus
der Realismus
der Nationalismus
der Marxismus
der Humanismus
der Anarchismus
der Darwinismus
der Opportunismus
der Optimismus
der Pessimismus

Practice 4 :

Most of the abstract nouns ending in -ik derive the agent by adding -er and the adjective by replacing the -ik with -isch. For each of the following abstract nouns give a related agent-noun and an adjective.

Model:

die Mechanik	der Mechaniker	mechanisch
die Mathematik	der Mathematiker	mathematisch

die Rhetorik
die Physik
die Methodik
die Analytik
die Graphik
die Metaphysik
die Pragmatik
die Botanik
die Statistik
die Technik
die Politik
die Klassik

Practice 5 :

Abstract nouns ending in -ie form the agent by dropping the -ie ending. Agents derived from nouns ending in -ogie end in -oge.

Model:

die Demokratie'	(-)	der Demokrat'	demokratisch
die Biologie'	(-e)	der Biologe	biologisch

```
die Diplomatie      (-)
die Biographie      (-)
die Ökonomie        (-)
die Geographie      (-)
die Fotografie      (-)
die Bürokratie      (-)
die Philosophie     (-)
die Philologie      (-e)
die Theologie       (-e)
die Psychologie     (-e)
```

Practice 6 :

For each of the following nouns give a related verb with the ending   -ieren
and its English meaning.

Model:

```
die Gratulation    (congratulation)      gratulieren   (to congratulate)
die Division       (division)            dividieren    (to divide)

die Demonstration
die Variation
die Qualifikation  (k becomes z)
die Konzentration
die Immigration
die Kolonisation
die Reservation
die Kombination
die Delegation
die Deklamation
die Klassifikation (k becomes z)
die Illumination
die Amputation
die Produktion     (k becomes z)
die Definition
die Polarisation
die Kulmination
```

NOTE: There are a few pitfalls that should be avoided. Some Latinic words in
German which sound like English words have a very different meaning. Beware
of these so-called "false friends":

```
        aktuell            topical (not actual)
        Distanz            aloofness (not distance)
        eventuell          possible (not eventual)
        exerzieren         drill ( not exercise)
        Fraktion           faction (not fraction)
        kontrollieren      check (not control)
        Konzern            firm or business (not concern)
        sensibel           sensitive (not sensible)
```

B. COMPOUNDS

Compound words are characteristic of German and are put together from a large variety of word components:

Kindergarten	(Noun	+ Noun)	eiskalt	(Noun	+	Adject.)
Schwarzwald	(Adjective	+ Noun)	mitlaufen	(Prep.	+	Verb)
Waschmaschine	(Verb	+ Noun)	freisprechen	(Adject.	+	Verb)

In English some compounds may be written as one word, i.e. icebox, railroad, mailman, but on the whole, separate words are preferred (potato salad, fire engine, to get up). In some instances a genitive construction is required to translate a German compound:

der Tagesbeginn   - the beginning of the day
die Relativitätstheorie   - theory of relativity

Compounds in general are formed when a pair or a group of independent words frequently used together in a normal grammatical relation are regarded and written as one word:

Grammatical Relation   Compound

die Lampe auf dem Tisch   die Tischlampe
the lamp on the table   the table lamp

die Reise nach Amerika   die Amerikareise
the trip to America   the America trip

Es ist so kalt wie Eis.   Es ist eiskalt.
It is as cold as ice.   It is ice cold.

I. COMPOUND NOUNS

1. Noun + Noun

The compound noun consists of a base noun, the last element, which is determined or made more precise by the limiting noun, the first element:

LIMITING NOUN	+	BASE NOUN	=	COMPOUND NOUN
der Tisch		die Lampe (-n)		die Tischlampe (-n)
die Kartoffel		der Salat (-e)		der Kartoffelsalat (-e)
der Sommer		das Kleid (-er)		das Sommerkleid (-er)

Note that the gender and the plural form of a compound noun are determined by the last component, the base noun.

German compounds are commonly understood when you try to find out what the parts mean. But sometimes the full word can be something different than just the sum of its parts. Even in cases like the following a knowledge of the parts will make the whole word a lot easier to remember:

LIMITING NOUN		BASE NOUN		COMPOUND NOUN
A der Sommer (summer)	+	B das Kleid (dress)	=	AB das Sommerkleid (summer dress)
A die Hand (hand)	+	B der Schuh (shoe)	=	C der Handschuh (glove)

Practice 7 :

Match the German compounds in each group with the English words on the right.

A. Limiting Noun "Haupt"

1. die Hauptstrasse
2. die Hauptstadt
3. die Hauptrolle
4. das Hauptwort
5. das Hauptfach

    a. capital city
    b. main road
    c. major, principal subject
    d. leading role
    e. noun, substantive

B. Limiting Noun "Haus"

1. die Hausschuhe
2. die Hausfrau
3. der Hausarzt
4. der Hauslehrer
5. die Hausaufgabe

    a. slippers
    b. homework
    c. family doctor
    d. private tutor
    e. housewife

C. Limiting Noun "Staat"

1. der Staatsbesuch
2. der Staatsdienst
3. das Staatsgebäude
4. die Staatswissenschaft
5. der Staatsbürger

    a. citizen
    b. civil service
    c. political science
    d. public building
    e. state visit

D. Limiting Noun "Welt"

1. die Weltlage
2. das Weltgericht
3. die Weltanschauung
4. die Weltreise
5. die Weltkugel

    a. globe
    b. international situation
    c. journey around the world
    d. last judgement
    e. view of life

Practice 8 :

Complete the following sentences, using one of the five compounds in the respective group.

A. 1. der Roman ist beim . . . . nicht mehr erhältlich.
    2. Unser . . . . hat den besten Salat.
    3. Die . . . . verkaufen immer mehr ausländische Wagen.

4. Ich bestelle ein Dutzend Rosen beim . . . .
5. Wieviel hast du beim . . . . für die Betten bezahlt ?

   a. Blumenhändler. b. Möbelhändler. c. Autohändler. d. Buchhändler.
e. Gemüsehändler.

B. 1. Diese Stadt kann ich auf der . . . . nicht finden.
    2. Für Goethes "Faust" sind schon alle . . . . . . ausverkauft.
    3. Herr Ober, bringen Sie uns bitte die . . . . !
    4. Mein Freund schrieb mir eine . . . . aus Paris.
    5. Eine . . . . auf der Strassenbahn ist nicht teuer.

   a. Wochenkarte. b. Theaterkarte. c. Speisekarte und Weinkarte.
d. Landkarte. e. Postkarte.

C. 1. Gib die Butter und Milch wieder in den . . . . !
    2. Die Diebe haben 2,000 Mark aus dem . . . . gestohlen.
    3. Die Hosen hängen im . . . .
    4. Nimm doch den Hammer aus dem . . . . !
    5. Das Lexikon habe ich wieder in den . . . . . . gestellt.

   a. Werkzeugschrank. b. Bücherschrank. c. Eisschrank. d. Geldschrank.
e. Kleiderschrank.

D. 1. Der Arzt hat ihn im . . . . operiert.
    2. Wir verbringen den Urlaub in unserem . . . .
    3. Der Bürgermeister gibt heute im . . . . einen Empfang.
    4. Sie haben sehr gut in diesem . . . . gegessen.
    5. Die Kinder spielen mit dem . . . .

   a. Landhaus. b. Krankenhaus. c. Puppenhaus. d. Rathaus. e. Gasthaus.

Practice 9 :

Complete the second statement with a compound noun as demonstrated in the model.

Model: Das Haus hat eine Haustür.   Der Garten hat eine . . . . .(Gartentür)
      Wir trinken Milch aus dem Milchglas. Wir trinken Bier aus dem . . . (Bierglas)

1. Die Goethestrasse ist nach Goethe benannt. Die . . . . . ist nach Mozart benannt.
2. Auf dem Tisch steht die Tischlampe. Auf dem Nachttisch steht die . . . .
3. Das Abendessen ist um 6 Uhr. Das . . . . . . ist um 12 Uhr.
4. Im Wohnzimmer stehen die Wohnzimmermöbel. Im Schlafzimmer stehen die . . . .
5. Für das Haar brauchen wir eine Haarbürste. Für die Kleider brauchen wir eine . . . .
6. Das Haus hat eine Hausnummer. Das Telefon hat eine . . . .
7. Die Studenten wohnen im Studentenheim. Die Kinder wohnen im . . . .
8. Die Gemüsesuppe wird aus Gemüse gemacht. Die . . . . . wird aus Reis gemacht.
9. Im Kleidergeschäft kauft man Kleider. Im . . . . kauft man Blumen.
10. Im Dorf steht die Dorfkirche. In der Stadt steht die . . . .

2. Connectives in Compound Nouns

In German, various connectives may appear in a compound. Compare the following combinations:

								CONNECTIVE
das Land	+	das Haus	=	das Landhaus	(country house)			none
das Land	+	der Mann	=	der Landsmann	(fellow countryman)			-s
das Land	+	der Herr	=	der Landesherr	(sovereign)			-es
das Land	+	die Kunde	=	die Länderkunde	(geography)			-er (plural)

a.) Simple compounds are formed by combining nouns with no ending on the limiting noun:

das Holz	+	der Schuh	=	der Holzschuh
das Stroh	+	der Hut	=	der Strohhut
der Kaffee	+	die Tasse	=	die Kaffeetasse

b.) The most frequently used connective -s or -es is understood as a genitive case ending on the limiting noun:

die Farben des Landes	=	die Landesfarben
das Licht des Himmels	=	das Himmelslicht
die Arbeit des Tages	=	die Tagesarbeit

The genitive ending -s often appears where it is grammatically out of place. Feminine nouns regularly remain unchanged in the singular:

das Fest der Weihnacht	=	das Weihnachtsfest
der Tag der Hochzeit	=	der Hochzeitstag
der Tag der Geburt	=	der Geburtstag

c.) Other compounds are formed by using the plural form of the limiting noun:

das Zimmer der Kinder	=	das Kinderzimmer
der Freund der Bücher	=	der Bücherfreund
der Rauch der Zigaretten	=	der Zigarettenrauch

Many feminine nouns tend to take an -en or -n connective in analogy to the plural ending -en:

der Schein der Sonne	=	der Sonnenschein
das Ende der Woche	=	das Wochenende
der Name der Strasse	=	der Strassenname

d.) Occasionally a portion of the first component is dropped:

der Westen	+	Deutschland	=	Westdeutschland
die Schule	+	das Haus	=	das Schulhaus

Unfortunately, no rules can be given for the use of the connectives. It has to be learned through practice. When in doubt, the student must consult a dictionary.

Form genitive compounds.

Model: das Alter des Kindes   -   das Kindesalter
        das Lied des Volk(e)s   -   das Volkslied

        die Regelung des Verkehrs
        das Haus Gottes
        der Bericht des Jahres
        die Zeit des Lebens
        das Rauschen des Waldes
        das Fenster der Wohnung   (add -s)
        die Grenze des Landes
        der Präsident des Bundes
        die Treue des Freundes
        der Wagen des Volk(e)s
        der Kapitän des Schiff(e)s
        der Leiter des Betrieb(e)s
        der Herr des Gut(e)s
        der Ausdruck des Gesicht(e)s

Practice 11 :

Match the German compounds with their English equivalents.

 1. die Arbeiterpartei   a. women's fashion
 2. das Liederbuch   b. cigarette smoker
 3. die Häuserreihe   c. coast guard
 4. die Studentenverbindung   d. coat hanger
 5. der Kleiderständer   e. crying of children
 6. der Zigarettenraucher   f. fraternity
 7. die Frauenmode   g. crowd of people
 8. die Küstenwache   h. row of houses
 9. die Menschenmenge   i. song book
10. der Männerverein   j. Labor Party
11. das Kindergeschrei   k. men's club
12. die Hundehütte   l. doghouse

Practice 12 :

Form two compound nouns of each noun pair according to the model. (Connectives
are indicated)

Model: das Haus   - der Garten   der Hausgarten   (house garden)
                                          das Gartenhaus   (the garden house)

        die Tasche(-n)- das Geld   das Taschengeld (the pocket money)
                                          die Geldtasche   (the wallet)

die Blume (-n)	-	der Topf
der Ball	-	das Spiel
das Land (-es)	-	der Feind (-es)
der Verkehr (-s)	-	die Strasse (-n)
der Baum	-	der Stamm
das Fleisch	-	die Suppe (-n)
die Höhe (-n)	-	der Flug
die Grenz(e)	-	das Gebiet (-s)
das Kleid(-er)	-	das Haus
der Tag (-es)	-	die Arbeit (-s)

3. Other Combinations of Compound Nouns

So far **only one structural** pattern has been treated, namely the combination of two or more nouns, which is the most productive type of word compounding. Other combinations, some of them less frequently employed, may be the following:

VERB STEM	+	NOUN			
schreib(en)	+	der Tisch	=	der Schreibtisch	(desk)
wohn(en)	+	der Wagen	=	der Wohnwagen	(trailer)
trink(en)	+	das Wasser	=	das Trinkwasser	(drinking water)

ADJECTIVE	+	NOUN *)			
schwarz	+	der Wald	=	der Schwarzwald	(Black Forest)
gross	+	die Mutter	=	die Grossmutter	(grandmother)
früh	+	das Jahr	=	das Frühjahr	(spring)

ADVERB	+	NOUN			
aussen	+	der Handel	=	der Aussenhandel	(foreign trade)
wieder	+	die Wahl	=	die Wiederwahl	(re-election)
wohl	+	der Stand	=	der Wohlstand	(prosperity)

NUMERAL	+	NOUN			
ein	+	das Horn	=	das Einhorn	(unicorn)
drei	+	das Rad	=	das Dreirad	(tricycle)
vier	+	das Eck	=	das Viereck	(quadrangle)

*)The adjective usually remains uninflected.

PREPOSITION	+	NOUN			
nach	+	der Mittag	=	der Nachmittag	(afternoon)
mit	+	die Arbeit	=	die Mitarbeit	(cooperation)
vor	+	das Spiel	=	das Vorspiel	(prelude)

Practice 13:

Form adjective-noun compounds and determine their meanings.

Model:
neu	-	die Zeit	die Neuzeit	(modern times)
gross	-	die Stadt	die Grosstadt	(metropolis)

Adjective	Noun
jung	die Frau
voll	der Mond
kurz	die Schrift
roh	die Seide
dumm	der Kopf
halb	die Insel
doppel	das Bett
hoch	die Schule
weiss	das Brot
frei	die Zeit
neu	das Jahr
rot	der Wein
schwarz	die Beere
gelb	der Filter
laut	der Sprecher
fern	der Schreiber
früh	der Sport
edel	der Mann

Practice 14:

Many German family and place names are compounds. Try to analyze the following names:

Salzburg	Vielbach	Hochfeld	Hochmüller
Obersalzberg	Königsstuhl	Niedertal	Jungwirt
Münsterland	Untermühl	Neumarkt	Altmann
Holzkirchen	Frauendorf	Altenmarkt	Neuberger
Kirchberg	Altenburg	Mönchsberg	Grossmann
Oberfelden	Ostsee	Frankenburg	Kleinschmied
Neustand	Hintersee	Rattenberg	Baumann

Practice 15 :

Match the German compounds with the English words on the right.

A.   1. das Fahrgeld   a. bicycle
      2. die Fahrprüfung   b. vehicle
      3. das Fahrzeug   c. passenger
      4. der Fahrgast   d. fare
      5. das Fahrrad   e. driving test

B.   1. die Schreibmaschine   a. spelling error
      2. die Schreibweise   b. stationery
      3. der Schreibfehler   c. typewriter
      4. der Schreibtisch   d. style of writing
      5. das Schreibpapier   e. desk

C.   1. das Sparbuch   a. savings account
      2. die Spareinlage   b. savings bank
      3. der Sparverein   c. savings deposit
      4. die Sparkasse   d. savings book
      5. das Sparkonto   e. savings club

D.   1. das Trinkgeld   a. drinking song
      2. der Trinkspruch   b. taproom
      3. die Trinkstube   c. tip
      4. das Trinklied   d. toast
      5. der Trinkbecher   e. drinking cup

Practice 16 :

Form verb-noun compounds from the word pairs provided and determine their meanings.

rasieren	-	der Apparat	binden	-	der Faden
nähen	-	die Nadel	kochen	-	der Topf
parken	-	der Platz	laufen	-	die Bahn
waschen	-	die Maschine	lehren	-	das Buch
trinken	-	das Wasser	treiben	-	der Stoff
reiten	-	die Schule	lernen	-	die Freiheit
stehen	-	die Lampe	braten	-	die Pfanne
tanken	-	die Stelle	wohnen	-	das Haus

Practice 17 :

Fill in the blanks with the corresponding verb-noun compounds.

Model: Das Zimmer, in dem wir wohnen, ist ein Wohnzimmer. (living room)
       Das Zimmer, in dem jemand stirbt, ist ein Sterbezimmer. (death-room)

   1. Das Zimmer, in dem die Kinder spielen, ist ein . . . .
   2. Das Zimmer, in dem wir studieren, ist ein . . . .

3. Das Zimmer, in dem wir essen, ist ein . . . .
4. Das Zimmer, in dem wir arbeiten, ist ein . . . . (-s connective)
5. Das Zimmer, in dem wir schlafen, ist ein . . . .
6. Das Zimmer, in dem wir lesen, ist ein . . . . (-e connective)
7. Das Zimmer, in dem wir baden, ist ein . . . . (-e connective)
8. Das Zimmer, in dem wir rauchen, ist ein . . . .
9. Das Zimmer, in dem wir warten, ist ein . . . . (-e connective)
10. Das Zimmer, in dem die Kranken sind, ist ein . . . .

Practice 18 :

Give the English meaning of the second word in each pair.

der Eingang *	(entrance)	-	der Ausgang	-
der Einwanderer	(immigrant)	-	der Auswanderer	-
die Einfuhr	(import)	-	die Ausfuhr	-
der Eindruck	(impression)	-	der Ausdruck	-
der Einblick	(insight)	-	der Ausblick	-
die Einreise	(entry)	-	die Ausreise	-
die Vorspeise	(appetizer)	-	die Nachspeise	-
der Vorname	(first name)	-	der Nachname	-
der Vormittag	(forenoon)	-	der Nachmittag	-
der Vorteil	(advantage)	-	der Nachteil	-
das Vorspiel	(prelude)	-	das Nachspiel	-
der Vorsommer	(early summer)		der Nachsommer	-
das Vorwort	(preface)	-	das Nachwort	-
der Vorderfuss	(forefoot)	-	der Hinterfuss	-
die Vorderachse	(front axle)	-	die Hinterachse	-
der Vordergrund	(foreground)	-	der Hintergrund	-
das Vorderrad	(front wheel)	-	das Hinterrad	-
der Vordersitz	(front seat)	-	der Rücksitz	-
die Vorderansicht	(front view)	-	die Rückansicht	-
die Vorderseite	(front)	-	die Rückseite	-

4. Grammatical Relationship Expressed In Compound Nouns

It has been pointed out before that the two elements of a compound stand
in a syntactical relationship to each other. This relation need not be
fully expressed. Thus, in the word "Zeigefinger" (index finger) the
limiting component, the verb "zeigen", denotes the purpose for which the
finger is used, namely for pointing. The limiting word can function as a
basis of comparison with the second element in the word "Bärenstimme"
(a voice like a bear).

In the following table we are going to examine more of these relationships
that can exist between the elements of a compound noun.

---

* The preposition "in" when used as a prefix becomes "ein".

Place or Direction:	Alpenflug (flight across the Alps)	- Flug über die Alpen
Time:	Sommerhitze (summer heat)	- Hitze im Sommer
Cause:	Hungertod (starvation)	- Tod aus (vor) Hunger
Result:	Todessturz (fatal plunge)	- Sturz in den Tod
Purpose:	Erholungsreise (recreational trip)	- Reise, um sich zu erholen
Means:	Hammerschlag (stroke with the hammer)	- Schlag mit dem Hammer
Manner:	Edelmann (nobleman)	- der edle Mann
Matter:	Eisentor (iron gate)	- Tor aus Eisen gemacht
Comparison:	Adlernase (eagle's nose)	- Er hat eine Nase wie ein Adler.
Possession:	Klostergarten (monastery garden)	- Der Garten gehört dem Kloster.
Apposition:	Strumpfhose (pantyhose)	- Strumpf + Hose

Practice 19 :

Express the grammatical relation by a compound noun. Note the given
connectives.

Model: ein Vogel, der im Wasser lebt   =   ein Wasservogel   (water bird)
       eine Reise zur Erholung(-s)   =   eine Erholungsreise (recreational trip)

    ein Weg, der durch den Wald führt
    ein Stern, der am Morgen leuchtet
    eine Pfanne zum Brat(en)
    eine Fahrt mit der Eisenbahn
    Lieder, die am Rhein gesungen werden
    ein Essen am Abend
    ein Platz zum Park(en)
    eine Treppe, die in den Keller führt
    die Arbeit in der Nacht
    eine Zeitung, die am Abend erscheint
    ein Hund für die Blinden
    eine Tür aus Glas
    der Haken für die Kleider
    die Säge, um Metall zu sägen
    Er hat eine Stimme wie ein Bär(-en).
    Das Land gehört dem Feind(-es).
    die roh(e) Seide

Give the approximate English meaning of the following compounds without consulting the dictionary.

1. der Fünfjahresplan	10. der Vierfarbendruck
2. der Zweitaktmotor	11. das Zwölfpunkteprogramm
3. der Dreikönigstag	12. das Siebenmonatskind
4. die Hundertjahrfeier	13. die Untergrundbahn
5. der Autobusbahnhof	14. die Mitternachtsstunde
6. die Fussballmeisterschaft	15. die Lebensversicherungsgesellschaft
7. der Autobahnbau	16. die Strassenverkehrsordnung
8. die Strassenbahnhaltestelle	17. die Weltraumforschung
9. die Arbeitslosenunterstützung	18. die Umweltverschmutzung

II. COMPOUND ADJECTIVES AND PARTICIPLES

Compound adjectives are composed of an adjective as a base and a limiting word as a second component. Also included in this chapter is the formation of compounds with a verbal adjective, i.e. a present or past participle. Compound adjectives assume the normal adjective ending when used before a noun.

Compound adjectives display a large variety of combinations:

NOUN		+ ADJECTIVE (PARTICIPLE)			
die See	(sea)	+ krank (sick)	=	seekrank	(seasick)
der Tod	(death)	+ sicher (sure)	=	todsicher	(sure as death, cocksure)
die Zeit	(time)	+ rauben (to rob)	=	zeitraubend	(time-consuming)
die Luft	(air)	+ kühlen (to cool)	=	luftgekühlt	(air-cooled)

ADJECTIVE		+ ADJECTIVE (PARTICIPLE)			
schwer	(serious)	+ krank (sick)	=	schwerkrank	(seriously ill)
taub	(deaf)	+ stumm (mute)	=	taubstumm	(deaf-mute)
weit	(far)	+ reichen (to reach)	=	weitreichend	(far-reaching)
frisch	(fresh)	+ backen (to bake)	=	frischgebacken	(freshly baked)

ADVERB		+ ADJECTIVE (PARTICIPLE)			
immer	(always)	+ grün (green)	=	immergrün	(evergreen)
ausser	(outside)	+ gewöhnlich (common)	=	aussergewöhnlich	(uncommon)
wohl	(well)	+ haben (to have)	=	wohlhabend	(well-to-do)
wohl	(well)	+ erziehen (to rear)	=	wohlerzogen	(well-bred)

VERB		+	ADJECTIVE				
loben	(to praise)	+	wert	(worthy)	=	lobenswert	(praiseworthy)
denken	(to think)	+	faul	(lazy)	=	denkfaul	(too lazy to think)

NUMERALS		+	ADJECTIVE (PARTICIPLE)				
vier	(four)	+	beinig (Bein-leg)	=	vierbeinig	(four-legged)
drei	(three)	+	eckig (angular)	=	dreieckig	(triangular)
viel	(much)	+	versprechen (promise)	=	vielversprechend (very promising)
alle	(all)	+	lieben (to love)	=	alliebend	(all-embracing)

PRONOUN		+	PARTICIPLE				
ich	(I)	+	beziehen (to refer)	=	ichbezogen	(self-centered)
selbst	(self)	+	machen (to make)	+	selbstgemacht	(self-made)

Some of these adjectival compounds occur with endings on the limiting
adjective, others do not. In general, connectives are less frequently used
with compound adjectives than with nouns.

1. Connectives

   Connective -s (-es) in analogy to the genitive ending:

das Blut	+ verwandt	=	blutsverwandt	(related)
der Geist	+ krank	=	geisteskrank	(mentally ill)
lieben	+ würdig	=	liebenswürdig	(lovable)
danken	+ wert	=	dankenswert	(worthy, deserving)

   Connectives -e, -er and -en in analogy to the plural endings:

der Hund	+ müde	=	hundemüde	(dog-tired)
das Kind	+ leicht	=	kinderleicht	(very easy, foolproof)
die Klasse	+ bewusst	=	klassenbewusst	(class-conscious)

2. Syntactical Relations

   Compound adjectives display a diversity of syntactical relationships:

staatsgefährlich	(subversive)	-	dem Staat gefährlich
eiskalt	(ice-cold)	-	so kalt wie Eis
schwerkrank	(seriously ill)	-	schwer (sehr) krank
stockdumm	(completely stupid)	-	äusserst dumm
denkfaul	(too lazy to think)	-	zu faul zu denken
alltäglich	(every day, common)	-	alle Tage (vorkommend)
lungenkrank	(consumptive)	-	krank an der Lunge
hitzebeständig	(heat-resistant)		gegen Hitze beständig

fleischfressend	(carnivorous)	-	es frisst Fleisch
umweltbedingt	(conditioned by environment)	-	durch die Umwelt bedingt
schmutzbedeckt	(covered with dirt)	-	mit Schmutz bedeckt
sonnengebräunt	(suntanned)	-	von der Sonne gebräunt
weltbekannt	(world-famous)	-	in der Welt bekannt
haftentlassen	(released from detention)	-	aus der Haft entlassen

3. Notes on Translating

For the most part, German adjectival and participial compounds have a parallel construction in English:

eine mondbeschienene Landschaft	a moonlit landscape
ein luftgekühlter Motor	an air-cooled motor
hartgekochte Eier	hard-boiled eggs
ein fabrikverschlossenes Paket	a factory-sealed package

However, it may be necessary to break up certain German modifying compounds into phrases and to place them after instead of before the noun, in order to get a smooth English translation:

ein federleichtes Kleid	a dress as light as a feather
ein diensthabender Offizier	an officer on duty
eine windgeschützte Bucht	a bay protected against the wind

Certain compounds do not allow a word-for-word translation in English at all:

ein feuerspeiender Berg	-	a vulcanic mountain	(vomiting fire)
eine wirklichkeitsnahe Politik	-	a realistic policy	(close to reality)
das ist naheliegend	-	that is obvious	(lying near)
schwerwiegende Folgen	-	grave consequences	(heavily weighing)
ein grundlegender Unterschied	-	a fundamental difference	(laying a base)

III. COMPOUND PARTICLES

Particles comprise adverbs, prepositions, and conjunctions, in short, all words that remain uninflected. Compound particles have developed in many ways and are not as easily understood from the meaning of their components as the compounds previously discussed. We give as examples only those compound particles that can be used as prefixes in compound verbs:

1. auseinander, entzwei	apart, asunder
miteinander, aneinander	together, jointly
übereinander	one upon another
gegeneinander	against one another
beiseite	aside, apart
gegenüber	opposite, across

empor	up, upwards
entgegen	towards; contrary to
voran, voraus	ahead
vorbei, vorüber	past, by; along
zurück	back, behind
zusammen	together

2. da- Compounds

darauf, drauf	on it
daneben	near it, next to it; besides
darüber, drüber	over, about, across it
darum	around, about it
darunter, drunter	under it; among them
davon	of, from it; away, off
davor	in front of it, before it
dazwischen	between, in between
dazu	to, for it; in addition to
dagegen	against it

3. Compounds with -wärts

aufwärts	upward(s), up
abwärts	downward(s), down
rückwärts	backward(s), back
vorwärts	forward, onward, on, ahead
auswärts	outward(s), out of doors
einwärts	inward(s)

4. Compounds with hin and her

See pages 28 and 31

Practice 21 :

Replace the adjectival phrase by a noun-adjective compound using the nouns
in parentheses.

Model: Ich bin **absolut** sicher.(Tod)   todsicher (dead sure)
    Das Badewasser war vollkommen kalt.(Eis) eiskalt (ice-cold)

Die Kinderstimmen klangen ganz hell. (Silber)
Das Flusswasser war völlig klar. (Kristall)
Die Aufgabe ist äusserst leicht. (Kinder)
Er war allen Studenten sehr hoch überlegen. (Turm)
Das Brot war völlig hart. (Stein)
Seine Spielschulden waren überaus gross. (Riesen)
Das Essen lag mir ziemlich schwer im Magen. (Blei)
Sein Gesicht war ganz schwarz. (Pech)
Das Auto fuhr überaus schnell. (Blitz)
Die Frau hatte eine sehr scharfe Zunge. (Messer)

Fill in the blank spaces with one of the five compounds corresponding to
the English expressions in parentheses.

A. 1. Sie hat . . . . (for years) auf seine Rückkehr gewartet.
    2. Er ist . . . . (for months) in Afrika gereist.
    3. . . . .(for weeks) hat sie schon nicht mehr angerufen.
    4. . . . .(for days) konnten wir nicht aus dem Haus gehen.
    5. Wir haben die Frau . . . . . . (for hours) weinen hören.

        a. tagelang b. stundenlang c. jahrelang d. wochenlang
        e. monatelang

B. 1. Seine Rede im Parlament war . . . . (significant).
    2. Der Direktor der Firma war . . . . (very busy).
    3. Zermatt ist ein . . . . (much frequented) Fremdenort in der
                                          Schweiz.
    4. Der Student war ein . . . . . . (promising) junger Mann.
    5. Der junge Autor war bereits eine . . . . . . (much talked-of)
                                         Persönlichkeit.

        a. vielgenannt b. vielsagend c. vielbesucht d. vielbeschäftigt
        e. vielversprechend

C. 1. Der Stoff ist . . . . (handwoven)
    2. Die Bilder auf der Vase sind . . . . (handpainted)
    3. Die Gläser sind . . . .(ground by hand)
    4. Der Brief ist . . . . . . (handwritten)
    5. Das Kleid ist . . . . . . (handmade)

        a. handgearbeitet b. handgeschliffen c. handgeschrieben
        d. handgemalt e. handgewebt

From the English words choose the fitting expression for each of the
German compound adjectives.

1.	lesenswert	a.	worth living
2.	hörenswert	b.	praiseworthy
3.	lobenswert	c.	pitiable
4.	beneidenswert	d.	worthy of imitation
5.	empfehlenswert	e.	worth mentioning
6.	bedauernswert	f.	enviable
7.	erwähnenswert	g.	worth hearing
8.	nachahmenswert	h.	deplorable
9.	beweinenswert	i.	worth recommending
10.	lebenswert	j.	worth reading

Form noun-adjective compounds using the present participle form from each
of the following verbs.

```
Model: die Zeit      - rauben     (time-consuming)   zeitraubend
       weit          - reichen    (far-reaching)     weitreichend

 1. der Fried(e)     - lieben      (peace-loving)
 2. das Silber       - glänzen     (silverlike)
 3. die Not          - leiden      (needy)
 4. der Grund        - legen       (fundamental)
 5. die Welt         - umspannen   (world-wide)
 6. der Dienst       - haben       (being on duty)
 7. das Aufsehen     - erregen     (sensational)
 8. die Gesundheit   - schädigen   (detrimental to health)
 9. die Post         - lagern      (general delivery)
10. die Gefahr       - drohen      (dangerous)
```

<u>Practice 25</u> :

Translate the following **German** phrases, using the given vocabulary.

```
Model: ein luftgekühlter Motor        (an air-cooled motor)
         die Luft - air
         kühlen    - to cool

       ein rauchgeschwärztes Zimmer   (a room black with smoke)
         der Rauch - smoke
         schwärzen - to blacken
```

```
 1. ein zorngerötetes Gesicht
      der Zorn - anger
      röten    - to redden

 2. eine bombenbeschädigte Stadt
      die Bombe    - bomb
      beschädigen  - to damage

 3. eine sonnenbeschienene Landschaft
      die Sonne   - sun
      bescheinen  - to shine upon

 4. ein kriegsverletzter Mann
      der Krieg - war
      verletzen - to injure

 5. ein holzgeschnitzter Altar
      das Holz   - wood
      schnitzen  - to carve

 6. ein goldverziertes Buch
      das Gold   - gold
      verzieren  - to decorate

 7. ein ferngelenktes Flugzeug
      fern   - remote
      lenken - to control

 8. ein heissgeliebtes Mädchen
      heiss - hot, ardent
      lieben - to love
```

IV. COMPOUND VERBS

Compound verbs present far less variety than compound nouns and adjectives. They may comprise verbs with a noun or adjective as first element, but are comparatively few in number. The first component is mostly separable.

1. Noun + Verb

achtgeben	(ich gebe acht)	to pay attention
stattfinden	(es findet statt)	to take place
preisgeben	(er gibt preis)	to abandon
skilaufen	(er läuft Ski)	to ski
radfahren	(ich fahre Rad)	to ride a bicycle
haltmachen	(sie machen halt)	to stop
teilnehmen	(er nimmt teil)	to take part
notlanden	(es notlandet)	to make an emergency landing

2. Adjective + Verb

fernsehen	(sie sehen fern)	to watch television
freisprechen	(ich spreche frei)	to acquit
festbinden	(er bindet fest)	to tie up
hochschätzen	(wir schätzen hoch)	to esteem highly
nassmachen	(sie machen nass)	to wet
fertigmachen	(ich mache fertig)	to finish
vollfüllen	(er vollfüllt)	to fulfill
vollfüllen	(er füllt voll)	to fill up

3. Particle + Verb (Separable Prefixes)

The most prolific group of compound verbs uses certain particles, frequently adverbs of location, that may form separable and inseparable prefixes. All of these prefixes have one or more standard meanings, and when joined to a certain verb, their meaning is simply added to it. Let us take for example the most ambiguous prefix um- , which may be associated with five different ideas, and see how it can affect the meaning of the verb. Only the context will determine its specific meaning within a sentence.

Prefix um-

a. "around" and "about"

Ein Gerücht geht um.   A rumor goes around.

b. "out of one's way" and "detour"

Wir müssen die Stadt umfahren.   We have to detour the town.

c. Notion of toppling and upsetting:

Der Sturm hat viele Bäume umgebrochen. The storm felled many trees.

d. "<u>again</u>", "<u>over</u>", "<u>re-</u>" and the idea of doing things in a different way:

Wir haben die Küche umgebaut.   We have remodeled the kitchen.

e. Indicates loss or deprivation:

Er ist in einem Unfall umgekommen. He was killed in an accident.

Listed below and on the following pages are the most common German prefixes together with their most frequent uses. It is very instructive to add them to a number of verbs in the accompanying table, and notice the various changes of meaning resulting from these combinations.

	-fahren	-geben	-kommen
ab- off, away; down	der Zug fährt um 6 Uhr ab - the train leaves at six o'clock	ein Paket abgeben- to deliver a parcel	von einer Gewohnheit abkommen - to discard a habit
an- at; on; to; approach, start	einen Hafen anfahren- to call at a port	den Preis angeben- to quote the price	er wird um 6 Uhr ankommen - he will arrive at six o'clock
auf- up; open; on	auf ein Strassen-hinderniss auffahren- run against a road-block	eine Stellung auf-geben- to give up a posi-tion	für den Schaden auf-kommen - to make good for the damage
aus- out of, from; notion of finishing	der Zug fährt aus - the train is pulling out	Befehle ausgeben - to issue orders	ich komme mit ihm aus- I get along with him
bei- by, with		dem Tee etwas Milch beigeben - to add milk to the tea	es ist ihm nicht bei-zukommen - he is inaccessible
durch- through, across; doing thoroughly	wir sind durchge-fahren - we drove through	die Nachricht durch-geben - to transmit the message	bei einer Prüfung durchkommen - to pass an examination

	-fahren	-geben	-kommen
ein- in, into; notion of getting used to	ein Auto einfahren - to break in a car	Medizin eingeben - to administer medi- cine	viel Geld ist einge- gangen - a lot of money has come in
entgegen- towards, contrary to			seinen Wünschen entgegenkommen - to meet his wishes
fort- away; notion of going on	bitte, fahren Sie fort ! - please go on !		von hier fortkommen - to get away from here
her- here, this way		Geld hergeben - to give away money	komm schnell her ! - come here quickly !
hin- there, that way	mit dem Bus hin- fahren - to go there by bus	sein Leben hingeben (für) - to give one's life for	wie komme ich hin ? - how do I get there ?
los- away; loose; notion of starting	er stieg ins Auto und fuhr los - he got into the car and drove away		von seiner Umgebung loskommen - to break away from one's environment
mit- with, along	lassen Sie mich mit- fahren - give me a ride	wir müssen ihm Essen mitgeben - we must provide him with food	ich werde mitkommen - I will come along
nach- after, after- ward; notion of imitating	ich fahre mit dem Auto nach - I will follow in my car	er gibt nicht nach - he won't give in	ich komme später nach - I will follow later
über- over, across	von einem Auto überfahren werden - to be run over by a car	er übergab mir den Brief - he handed me the letter	mich überkam die Angst - I was overcome by fear
um- (see page 26 section 3)	das Kap umfahren - to sail around the Cape	von Schwierigkeiten umgeben - beset by difficul- ties	in der Wüste umkommen - to perish in the desert

	-fahren	-geben	-kommen
unter- under, among; notion of finding shelter or cover		jemandem unter- geben sein - to be subordinated to a person	im Hotel unterkommen - to find accommodations in a hotel
vor- before; in front, ahead	links vorfahren - to pass on the left		das kommt selten vor - that occurs rarely
weg- away, gone	wir fahren heute abend weg - we are leaving tonight	gib es nicht weg ! - don't give it away !	er kam gut weg - he fared well
weiter- on, further, continue to	wir werden heute weiterfahren - we shall continue our trip today	geben Sie es weiter ! pass it on !	wie komme ich von hier weiter ? - how can I go on from here ?
wider- against, notion of reversal	was ist ihm wider- fahren ? - what has happened to him ?		
wieder- again		er gab es mir wieder - he returned it to me	kommen Sie wieder ! - come again !
zu- motion to (toward); idea of: addition closing duration acquiescence	fahr zu ! - drive on !	er will es nicht zugeben - he does not want to admit it	er kam auf mich zu - he came up to me
zurück- back, behind	ich fuhr im Autobus zurück - I rode back by bus	geben Sie die Zeitung zurück! - return the paper!	wir kommen spät zurück - we will come back late
zusammen- together	mit einem Auto zusammenfahren - to collide with a car		wir kommen morgen wieder zusammen - we will meet again tomorrow

4. Variable Prefixes

The majority of the prefixes listed in this table are separable prefixes. Only "durch", "über", "um", "unter", and "wieder" function both as separable and inseparable prefixes, depending upon stress and contextual meaning. When used in a literal sense, they are separated from the verb in the simple tenses and receive the word accent. When used in a figurative sense, they are never separated from the verb and not stressed.

Literal Sense (Separable)	Figurative Sense (Inseparable)
a. durchfliegen - fly through Die Maschine fliegt bis Rom durch.	durchfliegen - browse through, scan Er durchfliegt das Manuskript.
b. übergehen - go over Er geht zum Feind über.	übergehen - overlook Ich übergehe den Fehler.
c. umfahren - run down Ein Auto fuhr den Mann um.	umfahren - detour Wir umfahren die Stadt.
d. unterstehen - take shelter Wir stehen wegen des Regens unter.	unterstehen - be inferior, subordinate Alle diese Leute unterstehen mir.
e. wiederholen - go and get again Er holt es morgen wieder.	wiederholen - repeat Er wiederholte das Gesagte.

5. Semantic Relationship of Verbal Prefixes

Scanning through the long list of verbal prefixes, the reader will notice that a number of them are synonymous, i.e. they have the same meaning, while others can be grouped in pairs that express opposition or contradiction (antonyms).

a. Synonymous Prefixes:

The following prefixes indicate the idea of away, off, gone, lost, breaking up:

beiseite:	etwas beiseitebringen	- to remove something
davon:	Sachen davontragen	- to carry things away
ab:	ein Paket abschicken	- to send off a package
fort:	fortziehen	- march off, move, pull out
los:	den Hund losbinden	- to untie the dog
weg:	den Schmutz wegputzen	- to clean off the dirt

The prefixes an-, los-, auf- and ein- may express the notion of starting an action or doing it partially:

anbeissen (start biting, gnaw)   versus   abbeissen (bite off)

loslaufen (start running)

aufleuchten	(flash up)	= a sudden beginning
einfahren	**(break in a car)**	= a progressive beginning

The prefixes ab-, aus- and auf- may imply the notion of finishing an action, doing it thoroughly:

abbeissen	(bite off)
ausklingen	(cease to sound)
aufessen	(eat up)

The prefixes durch- and zu- may express duration:

durchschlafen	(sleep through)
zubringen	(spend time)

The prefixes an- and zu- convey the notion of approaching or being near by:

anschauen	(look at)
zukommen auf	(come up to)

b. Antonymical Prefixes:

abfliegen	(take off from the airport)	-	anfliegen	(approach the airport)
abrüsten	(disarm)	-	aufrüsten	(re-arm)
absteigen	(get off)	-	zusteigen	(get on)
anbinden	(tie)	-	losbinden	(untie)
aufmachen	(open)	-	zumachen	(close)
austreten	(leave)	-	eintreten	(enter)
nachlaufen	(run after)	-	vorlaufen	(run ahead)
unterbelichten	**(underexpose)**	-	**überbelichten**	**(overexpose)**

6. "Hin" and "Her" in Compound Separable Prefixes

Most of the prepositional prefixes of location have the ability to combine with the directional particles "hin" and "her", in order to convey the idea of specific motion in relation to the speaker or point of observation. Prefixes which may have several possible meanings when used alone always have one literal meaning when used with "hin" and "her". Compound prefixes are separable and the word accent falls on the second element.

Literal and Figurative Meanings (Simple Prefixes)	One Definite Meaning (Compound Prefixes)

<u>aus</u>gehen   a) to go out (on a date)
           b) to take a walk
           c) to end
           d) to run short
	<u>hinaus</u>gehen to go out(side)
	<u>heraus</u>gehen

<u>um</u>gehen   a) to go around
          b) to bypass
          c) to circulate
<u>um</u>gehen mit   d) keep company with
          e) to deal with
	<u>herum</u>gehen to go around

The most frequently used <u>hin-</u> and <u>her-</u> compound prefixes are:

herauf- on, up ← —————	hinauf- on, up ————— →
Sie kam die Treppe herauf. **She came up the stairs.**	Er ging die Treppe hinauf. He went up the stairs.

heraus- out ← —————	hinaus- out ————— →

Er holt die Schlüssel aus der
  Tasche heraus.
He takes the keys out of his
  pocket.
	Sie tragen die Sachen aus dem Zimmer
	  hinaus.
	They carry the things out of the
	  room.

herein- in(to) ← —————	hinein- in(to) ————— →
Bitte kommen Sie herein! Come in, please!	Die Kinder laufen ins Zimmer hinein. The children are running into the room.

herab-	down(ward)	hinab-	down(ward)
heran-	up to, near	hinan-	up to
herbei-	near, this way		
herüber-	over (here), across	hinüber-	over (there), across
herum-	around, about		
herunter-	under, down	hinunter-	under, down
hervor-	forth, out of	hinzu-	(up) to, in addition

Note that prefixes do not replace prepositions: aus...... hinaus, aus.....heraus, in.......hinein, in.......herein.

Practice 26 :

From the English words choose the fitting expressions for each of the German verb compounds.

1. bekanntmachen   a. to kill
2. sich breitmachen   b. to finish

3. fertigmachen	c. to turn and run
4. festmachen	d. to level
5. flüssigmachen	e. to compensate
6. gleichmachen	f. to make good, make up to
7. gutmachen	g. to stop
8. haltmachen	h. to empty
9. totmachen	i. to liquify
10. kehrtmachen	j. to make oneself comfortable
11. wiedergutmachen	k. to acquaint with
12. leermachen	l. to fix

Practice 27 :

In each of the following pairs of verbs an opposite notion is expressed. Give the English meaning of the second verb in each pair.

Model: ein Buch aufmachen   (to open) - zumachen   (to close)
       in ein Zimmer eintreten   (to enter) - austreten (to leave)

A. 1. Geld einzahlen   (deposit)   - auszahlen
    2. Fenster einhängen   (hinge)   - aushängen
    3. Truppen einschiffen   (embark)   - ausschiffen
    4. Koffer einpacken   (to pack)   - auspacken
    5. ins Auto einsteigen   (get in)   - aussteigen
    6. Luft einatmen   (breathe in) - ausatmen
    7. das Licht einschalten   (turn on)   - ausschalten
    8. die Wohnung einräumen   (put the
                           furniture in) - ausräumen
    9. Kaffee eingiessen   (pour)   - ausgiessen
    10. Waren einladen   (load)   - ausladen
    11. den Toten eingraben   (bury)   - ausgraben
    12. in die Stadt einmarschieren
                              (march   - ausmarschieren
                         into)
B. 1. den Vorhang aufziehen   (pull)   - zuziehen
    2. die Tür aufschliessen   (unlock)   - zuschliessen
    3. den Mantel aufknöpfen   (unbutton)   - zuknöpfen
    4. das Gas aufdrehen   (turn on)   - zudrehen
    5. den Teppich aufrollen   (unroll)   - zurollen
    6. den Deckel aufklappen   (open)   - zuklappen
    7. den Deckel aufdrücken   (press open) zudrücken
    8. die Schuhe aufschnallen   (unbuckle)   - zuschnallen
    9. ein Paket aufschnüren   (unlace,
                                     undo)   - zuschnüren
    10. eine Kiste aufschrauben   (unscrew)   - zuschrauben
    11. den Sack aufbinden   (untie)   - zubinden

C. 1. das Radio andrehen   (switch on) - abdrehen
    2. den Lautsprecher anstellen   (turn on)   - abstellen
    3. eine Verabredung ansetzen   (make, fix) - absetzen
    4. den Schmuck anlegen   (put on)   - ablegen
    5. ein Mitglied anmelden   (enroll a
                                     member)   - abmelden
    6. sich etwas angewöhnen   (to get
                                     used to)   - abgewöhnen

7. ein Kleid anziehen	(put on)	- ausziehen
8. ein Feuer anmachen	(make, build)	- ausmachen
9. auf die Strassenbahn auf- springen	(jump on)	- abspringen
10. im Theater auftreten	(make an appearance)	- abtreten
11. Waren aufladen	(load)	- abladen
12. auf das Pferd aufsteigen	(mount)	- absteigen
13. an Gewicht zunehmen	(gain weight)	- abnehmen
14. etwas zusagen	(promise, accept)	- absagen
15. Wasser fliesst zu	(flows in, towards)	- abfliessen
16. ein Foto überbelichten	(overexpose)	- unterbelichten
17. den Preis überbieten	(outbid)	- unterbieten
18. die Kraft überschätzen	(overestimate)	- unterschätzen
19. er ist überlegen	(superior)	- unterlegen
20. einem Auto vorfahren	(pass a car)	- nachfahren
21. die Uhr vorstellen	(set ahead)	- nachstellen
22. Truppen rücken vor	(advance)	- nachrücken

Practice 28 :

The prepositions **ab-**, **davon-**, **beiseite-**, **fort-** and **weg-**, which are used in the compound verbs below, express the idea of "away", "off" and "gone". Translate the sentences into English.

1. Bitte stelle den Motor ab. 2. Hast du deine Prüfungsarbeit schon abgegeben ? 3. Das Schreiben habe ich an seine Adresse abgeliefert. 4. Mir ist ein Knopf (button) abgegangen. 5. Er schiebt (pushes) die anderen gern beiseite. 6. Der Lehrer ruft den Schüler beiseite. 7. Ich lege mir das Geld fürs Alter beiseite. 8. Das Auto ist mit abgeblendeten (dimmed) Lichtern davongefahren. 9. Wir sind noch einmal davongekommen. 10. Der Dieb machte sich eiligst davon. 11. Das Kind ist den Eltern davongelaufen. 12. Ich lasse Sie nicht so bald fort. 13. Ich hoffe, dass wir rechtzeitig von hier fortkommen. 14. Die Truppen werden morgen wieder fortziehen. 15. Er hat mir die Autoschlüssel weggenommen. 16. Die Kinder legten ihr Spielzeug weg und halfen der Mutter. 17. Sie blickte weg, als sie ihn sah. 18. Der Zug ist vor wenigen Minuten weggefahren. 19. Das Schiff hat sich vom Anker losgerissen. 20. Er stieg ins Auto und fuhr los.

Practice 29 :

Choose the proper prefix so that the German compound with "machen" matches the English verb in parenthesis.

1. Er hat das Schild von der Tür ....-gemacht (remove). 2. Können Sie mir den Schrank an die Wand ....-machen (put on) ? 3. Machen Sie bitte ein Fenster ....(open)! 4. Wir haben das Feuer .... -gemacht (put out). 5. Der Student hat alle Klassen ....-gemacht (complete). 6. Meine Mutter hat frisches Obst ....-gemacht (can). 7. Die Jungen haben sich schnell ....-gemacht (leave). 8. Sie haben sich an ihn ....-gemacht (approach). 9. Das Mädchen hat sich sehr ....-gemacht(develop). 10. Du brauchst ihm nicht alles ....-zumachen (imitate). 11. Tausende von Soldaten wurden ....-gemacht (kill).

12. Er hat ihr sein Vermögen ....-macht (bequeath). 13. Wir haben
ein Brett ....-gemacht (put before).

a. vormachen b. anmachen c. ausmachen d. einmachen e. sich
herausmachen f. niedermachen g. nachmachen h. sich davonmachen
i. übermachen j. abmachen k. durchmachen l. aufmachen m. sich
heranmachen

Practice 30 :

Choose the proper prefix so that the German compound with "gehen" matches
the English verb in parenthesis.

1. Geht deine Uhr ....(be fast) ? 2. Du kannst ....gehen (go ahead)
und ich komme nach. 3. Leider geht nicht genug Geld .... (come in).
4. Der Koffer ist schon zu voll, er geht nicht .... (close). 5. Es
ist erst sieben Uhr. Ihre Uhr geht .... (be slow). 6. Viele Soldaten
sind ins feindliche Lager ....gegangen (go over). 7. Ich habe etwas
vergessen. Ich muss nochmals .... gehen (go back). 8. Ich fürchte,
das wird nicht gut .... gehen (end). 9. Er ist vom rechten Wege ....
gegangen (go astray). 10. Gehen Sie doch .... (go out). 11. Meine
Freunde haben mich ....gangen (deceive). 12. Der Angestellte ist mit
dem Geld ....gegangen (run away). 13. Das geht Sie nichts ....(concern).
14. Der Lehrer kann mit den Kindern nicht .... gehen (handle). 15. Die
Sonne geht im Winter sehr früh ....(set). 16. Meine Freundin ist so-
eben .... gegangen (pass by). 17. Soll ich auch .... gehen (come
along) ? 18. Ein plötzliches Gewitter ging .... (come down).

a. angehen b. zurückgehen c. vorgehen d. umgehen e. übergehen
f. vorausgehen g. eingehen h. abgehen i. untergehen j. vorbei-
gehen k. hinausgehen l. zugehen m. nachgehen n. hintergehen
o. mitgehen p. niedergehen q. durchgehen r. ausgehen

Practice 31 :

Give the English meanings of the compound verbs.

A. Notion of Approaching

1.	kommen	(to come)	ankommen
2.	rufen	(to call)	anrufen
3.	nehmen	(to take)	annehmen
4.	hören	(to hear)	anhören
5.	binden	(to tie)	anbinden
6.	liegen	(to lie)	anliegen
7.	schrauben	(to screw)	anschrauben
8.	sprechen	(to talk, to speak)	ansprechen
9.	wachsen	(to grow)	anwachsen
10.	greifen	(to grasp)	angreifen

B. Notion of Starting or Doing Partially

1.	laufen	(to run)	anlaufen
2.	heizen	(to heat)	anheizen
3.	fressen	(to eat)	anfressen
4.	sägen	(to saw)	ansägen
5.	braten	(to roast)	anbraten
6.	lernen	(to learn)	anlernen
7.	schneiden	(to cut)	anschneiden
8.	fangen	(to catch)	anfangen
9.	brechen	(to break)	anbrechen
10.	**fahren**	**(to go, drive)**	**anfahren**

C. Idea of Finishing Something or Doing Something Thoroughly

1.	**sperren**	**(to shut, close)**	**absperren**
2.	Anzug tragen	(to wear a suit)	abtragen
3.	schneiden	(to cut)	abschneiden
4.	brechen	(to break)	abbrechen
5.	fressen	(to eat)	abfressen
6.	arbeiten	(to work)	aufarbeiten
7.	füttern	(to feed)	auffüttern
8.	füllen	(to fill)	auffüllen
9.	pumpen	(to pump)	aufpumpen
10.	wühlen	**(to dig, rummage)**	aufwühlen
11.	trinken	(to drink)	austrinken
12.	giessen	(to pour)	ausgiessen
13.	essen	(to eat)	ausessen
14.	dienen	(to serve)	ausdienen
15.	lernen	(to learn)	auslernen

C. WORD DERIVATION

Along with the mastery of the etymological relationships and word compounding, the understanding of German prefixes, suffixes and other word building elements is the quickest and surest way of expanding the students' vocabulary methodically. The process of combining independent words, or their stems, with prefixes and suffixes which have no independent existence as words is called word derivation.

"Käufer"   (buyer, purchaser) is a derivative formed by adding the suffix
            -er to "kauf" (the stem of "kaufen").

"Kauf"   (purchase), the capitalized verb stem, is another noun derived
            from "kaufen".

"käuflich" (purchasable) is an adjective formed by adding the formative
            element -lich to the stem.

The prefix ver- alters the meaning of the verb "kaufen" and its derivatives in a certain predictable way, which results in four more new words:

verkaufen	- to sell	der Verkäufer	- salesman
der Verkauf	- the sale	verkäuflich	- for sale, vendible

When a student has mastered all the affixes and a basic vocabulary of about a thousand words, he can by means of exercises developed in the text acquire several thousand words with ease. In even rich languages like German with hundreds of thousands of words, the number of word-roots is relatively small. To know all the words of a language is clearly impossible ; to know most of its roots as well as all its prefixes and suffixes is possible.

I. FORMATION OF WORDS THROUGH SUFFIXES AND DERIVATIVE ALTERATIONS.

1. Infinitives Used As Nouns

Many German infinitives can be used as nouns to express the act of carrying out the action of the verb. Such nouns are usually equivalent to English gerunds. They are always neuter.

rauchen	- to smoke	das Rauchen	- smoking
wohnen	- to live	das Wohnen	- living
fahren	- to drive, ride	das Fahren	- driving, riding
lachen	- to laugh	das Lachen	- laughing, laughter
einsteigen	- to get on, board	das Einsteigen	- boarding, getting on
einkaufen	- to shop	das Einkaufen	- shopping

Some of these verbal infinitives have become nouns in their own right:

das Essen	eating; food; meal
das Leben	living; life
das Schreiben	writing; the letter
das Wissen	knowing; knowledge
das Aussehen	appearing; appearance
das Können	knowledge; skill
das Dasein	existence

The verbal infinitive can even function as the last component of a compound noun:

das Abendessen	supper
das Kopfzerbrechen	pondering, headache, racking one's brains
das Unterwasserschwimmen	swimming under water

Practice 32 :

Match the German kommen- compounds with the English words on the right.

1. das Abkommen	a. occurrence
2. das Ankommen	b. returning
3. das Aufkommen	c. agreement
4. das Auskommen	d. arriving
5. das Einkommen	e. income
6. das Fortkommen	f. competency, living
7. das Umkommen	g. shelter
8. das Unterkommen	h. perishing, dying
9. das Vorkommen	i. progress, getting on
10. das Wiederkommen	j. rise, advent

Practice 33 :

Translate the following sentences into English.

1. Das Singen und Lärmen ist verboten.
2. Das Überschreiten der Geleise (rail tracks) ist verboten.
3. Das Vorfahren in Kurven ist verboten.
4. Rauchen verboten.
5. Das Betreten des Rasens (lawn) ist verboten.
6. Das Öffnen der Fenster ist verboten.
7. Das Sprechen mit dem Fahrer ist verboten.
8. Das Schwimmen und Baden in diesem Fluss ist verboten.
9. Das Anlehnen der Fahrräder ist verboten.
10. Das Essen von mitgebrachten Speisen ist verboten.

2. Verbal Stems Used As Nouns

   a. Infinitive Stems

   A large number of nouns can be formed from verbal stems. Most of them are monosyllabic nouns. Note that there is a slight difference between stem-nouns and infinitive-nouns:

		Result of Action		Action	
drucken	(print)	der Druck	(print)	das Drucken	(printing)
bauen	(build)	der Bau	(building structure)	das Bauen	(building)
fallen	(fall)	der Fall	(fall, downfall)	das Fallen	(falling)
streiten	(argue)	der Streit	(argument)	das Streiten	(arguing)

rauchen	(smoke)	der Rauch	(smoke)	das Rauchen	(smoking)
blicken	(look, glance)	der Blick	(look, view)	das Blicken	(looking)
tanzen	(dance)	der Tanz	(dance)	das Tanzen	(dancing)
fangen	(catch)	der Fang	(catch)	das Fangen	(catching)
kaufen	(buy)	der Kauf	(purchase)	das Kaufen	(buying)
dampfen	(steam)	der Dampf	(steam)	das Dampfen	(steaming)

The following stem-nouns are formed by dropping the umlaut:

grüssen	(greet)	-	der Gruss	(greeting)
küssen	(kiss)	-	der Kuss	(kiss)
höhnen	(sneer, mock)	-	der Hohn	(scorn, sneer)
schämen	(be ashamed)	-	die Scham	(shame)
stürzen	(fall, tumble)	-	der Sturz	(fall, crash)
wählen	(choose, elect)	-	die Wahl	(choice, election)
wünschen	(wish)	-	der Wunsch	(wish)
zählen	(count)	-	die Zahl	(number, figure)

Stem-nouns can be formed from prefixed verbs in the same manner:

anfangen	(begin)	-	der Anfang	(beginning)
befehlen	(order, command)	-	der Befehl	(order, command)
besitzen	(own)	-	der Besitz	(property)
besuchen	(visit)	-	der Besuch	(visit)
empfangen	(receive)	-	der Empfang	(reception)
gewinnen	(win)	-	der Gewinn	(profit, gain)
versuchen	(try)	-	der Versuch	(attempt, trial)

b. Stem-Nouns of Strong Verbs

Other types of stem-nouns are formed by utilizing the stem of the principal parts of strong verbs, especially their past stem.

INFINITIVE	PAST	PAST PARTICIPLE
wachsen (grow)	wuchs	gewachsen
	der Wuchs (growth)	

beissen	(bite)	-	der Biss	(bite)
brennen	(burn)	-	der Brand	(fire)
greifen	(touch, seize)	-	der Griff	(grip, handle)
messen	(measure)	-	das Mass	(measure)
klingen	(sound)	-	der Klang	(sound)
reissen	(tear, rip)	-	der Riss	(tear)
schneiden	(cut)	-	der Schnitt	(cut)
schreiten	(stride, step)	-	der Schritt	(step, pace)
stehen	(stand)	-	der Stand	(stand, position)
treiben	(drive)	-	der Trieb	(drive)
zwingen	(force, coerce)	-	der Zwang	(coercion, compulsion)

INFINITIVE	PAST	PAST PARTICIPLE
finden (find)	fand	gefunden
		der Fund (finding)

binden	(bind, tie)	- der Bund	(band, union, league)
gehen	(go, walk)	- der Gang	(walk, gait, course)
schwinden	(dwindle, disappear)	- der Schwund	(dwindling, shrinkage)
schwingen	(swing)	- der Schwung	(pep, impetus)
trinken	(drink)	- der Trunk	(drink, potion)
springen	(spring, jump)	- der Sprung	(jump, leap)

c. Stem-Nouns of Strong Verbs with Modified Stem Vowel

The "o" of the past stem or past participle may be replaced by "u".
This change of stem vowel is called "Ablaut".

INFINITIVE	PAST
ziehen (pull, draw)	zog
	o 〉 u
	der Zug (pull, draught, train, trait)

brechen	(break)	- der Bruch	(breach, fracture)
fliegen	(fly)	- der Flug	(flight)
fliessen	(flow)	- der Fluss	(flow, river, stream)
geniessen	(enjoy)	- der Genuss	(enjoyment)
giessen	(pour, cast)	- der Guss	(downpour, casting)
schiessen	(shoot)	- der Schuss	(shot)
schliessen	(close, finish)	- der Schluss	(end, conclusion)
schwören	(swear)	- der Schwur	(oath)
sprechen	(speak, talk)	- der Spruch	(saying, sentence)

Practice 34 :

Complete the sentences by inserting a stem-noun derived from the verbs in parentheses.

1. Jetzt ist das . . . . aber voll. (messen)
2. Schliess das Fenster! Ich sitze nicht gern im . . . . . (ziehen)
3. In Amerika wird die . . . . . . aus der Stadt immer stärker. (fliehen)
4. Der . . . . . . nach Deutschland dauert nur mehr acht Stunden. (fliegen)
5. Ein kurzer . . . . . . und er war über die Hecke. (springen)
6. Mit . . . . . . werden Sie nichts erreichen. (zwingen)
7. Der . . . . . . eines Versprechens ist unethisch. (brechen)
8. Er tötete ihn mit einem . . . . . (schiessen)
9. Jetzt machen wir aber . . . . . (schliessen)
10. Sie haben den . . . . . . fürs Leben geschlossen. (binden)
11. Der . . . . . . der Kaufkraft macht der Bevölkerung Sorge. (schwinden)

12. Möchten Sie mit mir einen . . . . . . durch die Stadt machen. (gehen)
13. Den . . . . . . an der Tür muss ich noch putzen. (greifen)
14. Der Pflanzen- . . . . in der Arktis ist sehr gering. (wachsen)

Practice 35 :

Form masculine stem-nouns and give their English meanings.

1. ärgern	(make angry, annoy)	11. raten	(advise)	
2. bannen	(banish)	12. schreien	(scream, cry)	
3. danken	(thank)	13. scherzen	(make fun, joke)	
4. feiern	(celebrate) (=femin.)	14. schlagen	(beat, strike)	
5. handeln	(trade)	15. spalten	(split)	
6. heiraten	(marry) (=femin.)	16. spotten	(mock, scoff)	
7. kleiden	(dress, clothe) (=neuter)	17. sitzen	(sit)	
8. kämpfen	(fight)(drop umlaut)	18. teilen	(part, divide)	
9. laufen	(run)	19. wundern	(wonder, be surprised) (=neuter)	
10. loben	(praise) (=neuter)	20. wüten	(rage) (=femin.) (drop umlaut)	

Practice 36 :

Form stem-nouns in accordance with the model.

Model: Das, was man geniesst, ist ein Genuss.
Das, was man wünscht, ist ein Wunsch.

1. Das, was man fängt, ist ein . . . . .
2. Das, was man wählt, ist eine . . . . .
3. Das, was man schwört, ist ein . . . . .   (-u-)
4. Das, was man gewinnt, ist ein . . . . .
5. Das, was man baut, ist ein . . . . . .
6. Das, was fliesst, ist ein . . . . .   (-u-)
7. Das, was man kauft, ist ein . . . . .
8. Das, was man besitzt, ist ein . . . . .

d. Unusual Verb-Noun Derivation

Similar in nature to the aforementioned stem-nouns are those derivatives that
use the principal parts of strong verbs as a basis, but otherwise form the nouns
in different ways, especially by the addition of the suffix -e or -t
and sometimes by utilization of certain vowel changes. This group is not
too prolific; however, it is most remarkable for its tendency to form
compounds. In fact, two of these derivatives, "-nahme" and "-kunft" ,
can only occur in compounds. Note that they are all feminine.

Addition of the Suffix "-e" to the Stem-Noun:

binden	(bind, tie)	die Bande	(band, gang)
fahren	(drive)	die Fuhre	(cart-load)
helfen	(help)	die Hilfe	(help, assistance)
geben	(give)	die Gabe	(gift)
graben	(dig)	die Grube	(pit, mine)
nehmen	(take)	-nahme as in "Ausnahme" (exception)	
liegen	(lie, be situated)	die Lage	(situation, position)
sprechen	(speak)	die Sprache	(language)
steigen	(climb)	die Stiege	(stairs)
schneiden	(cut)	die Schnitte	(slice, cut)

Addition of the Suffix "-t" to the Stem-Noun:

fahren	(drive, ride, go)	die Fahrt	(drive, ride, trip)
		die Furt	(ford)
fliehen	(flee)	die Flucht	(flight)
graben	(dig)	die Gruft	(tomb)
haben	(have)	die Haft	(detention)
können	(can)	die Kunst	(art)
kommen	(come)	-kunft as in "Ankunft" (arrival)	
nähen	(sew)	die Naht	(seam, joint)
schreiben	(write)	die Schrift	(writing, script)
sehen	(see)	die Sicht	(sight)
tragen	(wear)	die Tracht	(costume, dress)
ziehen	(breed, cultivate)	die Zucht	(breeding, cultivation)

The student may be helped by studying the following table of nouns that are formed by combining some of these modified stem-nouns with prefixes. A comparison with the list of verbs on pages 27 to 29 will show that the basic meaning of such nouns coincides with the meaning of the verbs, e.g.

    "Abgabe" (delivery)   "abgeben" (deliver)

e. List of Compound Stem-Nouns

see next page

	a) -fahrt b) -fuhr	a) -gabe b) -(gift)	-gang	-nahme	-sicht	-stand
Ab-	a) departure b) removal, brushoff	delivery; tax	departure, leaving; retirement	taking off, decrease	intention, purpose	distance, interval
An-	a) arrival, approach b) supply	declaration, statement; instruction	--	acceptance, adoption; assumption	sight, view; opinion	decency, decorum
Auf-	a) ascent; drive	assignment, task	ascent; rising; staircase	reception; admission	supervision, inspection	uprising, revolt
Aus-	a) departure, drive b) export	delivery; expense; issue	exit; outlet	exception	view, outlook, prospect	strike, walkout
Bei-	--	addition, supplement	--	--	--	assistance
Durch-	a) passage b) transit	passing	passage, transit	going over, (through)	looking over, examination	--
Ein-	a) entrance, gateway b) import	application, petition	entry, entrance; receipt	taking, capture; receipt	insight; inspection	entrance
Fort-	--	--	departure; progress	--	--	--
Gegen-	--	--	--	--	--	object, topic, subject
Hin-	a) drive there, journey there	devotion	--	taking, putting up with	regard, respect	--
Her-	a) return trip	--	course of events	--	--	--
Mit-	a) traveling along	(Mitgift) dowry	--	taking along	--	--

	a) -fahrt b) -fuhr	-gabe -(gift)	-gang	-nahme	-sicht	-stand
Nach-	a) -- b) --	--	--	C.O.D.(collect on delivery)	indulgence	--
Nieder-	--	--	decline	--	--	--
Rück-("Zurück" for compound verbs)	a) return, return trip	giving back, returning, restitution	regress, recession	taking back,	regard, consideration	backlog; residue
Über-	a) crossing, passage b) ferry	delivery, handing over, surrender	crossing; transition	taking over	survey, summary	--
Um-	--	--	rotation; procession; relation	--	circumspection; wariness, caution	circumstance
Unter-	--	--	setting; ruin, downfall	--	--	shelter, dugout
Vor-	a) right of way	points or odds	process, proceedings	undertaking	(pre-)caution, care	head; board of directors; principal
Voraus-	--	--	--	--	foresight	--
Weg-	--	--	departure	taking away, seizure	--	--
Wider-	--	--	--	--	--	resistance, opposition
Wieder-	--	restitution; reproduction	--	--	--	--
Zu-	a) approach, access b) supply	addition, extra-	access, entrance, entry	increase, growth	--	condition, state

Note that the meaning of a noun so derived may differ from the meaning of the
infinitive-noun:

     die Auskunft   (information, inquiry) : das Auskommen (competency, living)
     der Vorgang   (process)   : das Vorgehen   (proceeding, action)

The two meanings coincide in:

     die Unterkunft
     das Unterkommen   (accommodation, lodging)

     die Einkünfte
     das Einkommen   (income, revenue)

Practice 37 :

Match the German compounds with the English words on the right.

1. der Umbau	a. overthrow, upheaval
2. der Umfang	b. looking around, lookout
3. der Umhang	c. envelope; change
4. die Umkehr	d. outline, contour
5. der Umlauf	e. turnover
6. der Umlaut	f. circulation, rotation
7. der Umriss	g. vowel change
8. der Umsatz	h. return
9. die Umschau	i. circumstance
10. der Umschlag	j. cape, wrap
11. die Umsicht	k. caution
12. der Umstand	l. rebuilding, reconstruction
13. der Umsturz	m. circumference; extent

Practice 38 :

Complete the sentences by inserting the German noun that corresponds to the
English word in parenthesis.

1. Das war ein wichtiger . . . . . in meinem Leben. (segment)
2. Der . . . . . . zwischen den Häusern ist nicht gross genug. (distance)
3. Meine Eltern haben eine sehr moderne . . . . . . von diesen Dingen. (outlook)
4. Der . . . . . der zerstörten Stadt ist nahezu abgeschlossen. (reconstruction)
5. Im Dezember haben wir viele . . . . . gehabt. (expenses)
6. Ohne ihren . . . . . könnten wir das nicht tun. (assistance)
7. Haben Sie die . . . . . im Radio gehört ? (announcement)
8. Ich habe sehr wenig . . . . . auf diesen Menschen. (influence)
9. Haben Sie gute . . . . . + -e (plural) gemacht ? (progress)
10. Über welchen . . . . haben Sie gesprochen ? (topic, subject)
11. Dieser Stoff ist englischer . . . . .   (origin)
12. Darf ich Sie um Ihre . . . . . bitten ? (cooperation)
13. Ich will das Paket als . . . . . schicken. (C.O.D)
14. Der . . . . . des römischen Reiches begann im 3. Jahrhundert. (downfall)

15. Du musst auf Dein Alter . . . . . . nehmen. (consideration)
16. Man merkt hier kaum den . . . . . . von Herbst zu Winter. (transition, change)
17. Ein berühmtes Buch von Knigge heisst ". . . . . . mit Menschen". (social intercourse)
18. Für die . . . . . in diesem Hotel zahlte ich nur 10 Mark. (accommodation)
19. . . . .! Da kommt ein Auto. (caution)
20. Wir fürchten die . . . . . nicht. (future)

  a. die Durchsage b. die Zukunft c. die Vorsicht d. der Abschnitt
  e. die Nachnahme f. der Niedergang g. die Rücksicht h. der Umgang
  i. die Unterkunft j. der Übergang k. der Einfluss l. der Aufbau
  m. die Anschauung n. die Ausgaben o. die Fortschritte p. der Gegenstand
  q. der Beistand r. die Mitarbeit s. die Herkunft t. der Abstand

3. Suffixes in English and German

English and German nouns are marked by a large number of derivational suffixes. In part they are similar in the two languages. Compare:

work	-	work__er__	Arbeit	-	Arbeit__er__
open	-	open__ing__	öffnen	-	Öffn__ung__
child	-	child__hood__	Kind	-	Kind__heit__
friend	-	friend__ship__	Freund	-	Freund__schaft__
king	-	king__dom__	König	-	König__tum__
wild	-	wilder__ness__	wild	-	Wild__nis__

The following pages are devoted to the use and analysis of the various German suffixes and prefixes, with emphasis on those that are most productive. The use of affixes for combination with existing words is the most important method of word making. The knowledge offered here is passive, and will not allow a student to form new words himself.

4. Formation of Nouns by Means of Suffixes

a. The Suffix "-e"

The suffix -e is used on verb stems and adjectives to form feminine nouns.

a 1. Nouns from Verbs

decken	-	die Decke	cover	-	cover, blanket
falten	-	die Falte	fold	-	fold, crease
folgen	-	die Folge	follow	-	sequence, consequence
pfeifen	-	die Pfeife	whistle	-	whistle, pipe
reden	-	die Rede	speak	-	speech
schrauben	-	die Schraube	screw	-	screw
sorgen	-	die Sorge	care	-	care
speisen	-	die Speise	have a meal-	meal
sperren	-	die Sperre	lock, block-	block, gate
suchen	-	die Suche	search	-	search

- 46 -

absagen	- die Absage	cancel	- cancellation
anzeigen	- die Anzeige	notify	- notice
einreisen	- die Einreise	enter	- entry
		(a country)	
nachfolgen	- die Nachfolge	succeed	- succession
vorhersagen	- die Vorhersage	predict	- prediction
zusagen	- die Zusage	promise	- promise

Nouns ending in -e may denote names of places where the action indicated in the verb takes place:

Der Schmied arbeitet in der Schmiede. (blacksmith's shop)
Das Vieh weidet auf der Weide. (pasture)

Note: See also Chapter 2. d. on page 42.

a 2. Nouns from Adjectives

These are abstract nouns indicating quality, state, or condition.
They take an Umlaut if possible.

bloss	- die Blösse	bare, naked-	bareness, nakedness
gross	- die Grösse	great, large-	greatness, largeness; size
hoch	- die Höhe	high	- height
kühl	- die Kühle	cool	- coolness
leer	- die Leere	empty	- emptiness
nass	- die Nässe	wet, moist -	moisture
reif	- die Reife	mature, ripe-	maturity, ripeness
schwarz	- die Schwärze	black	- blackness
stark	- die Stärke	strong	- strength
treu	- die Treue	faithful,	
		loyal	- faithfulness, loyalty

Note: Careful distinction should be made between nouns so derived and
adjective-nouns which retain adjective endings throughout:

der Arme	- the poor man	die Reichen	- the rich people
ein Fremder	- a stranger	die Deutschen	- the Germans
das Gute	- the good	etwas Wichtiges	- something important

Practice 39 :

For each of the following verbs give a related noun ending in -e, and its
English meaning.

bitten	(ask, request)
fragen	(ask, question)
glauben	(believe) **Exception: masculine gender**
lehren	(teach)
lügen	(lie)
pflegen	(take care of, attend)
aussagen	(state, declare)
anklagen	(accuse, indict)
auslesen	(pick out, select)
nachfragen	(ask, inquire)

From each of the following adjectives form nouns and change the sentences in accordance with the model. These nouns take an umlaut if possible.

Model: Das Buch ist dick.   - die <u>Dicke</u> des Buches   (the thickness)
       Der Fluss ist breit. - die <u>Breite</u> des Flusses (the width)

    1. Das Leben ist kurz.   (-"-)
    2. Die Arbeit ist schwer.
    3. Die Natur ist still.
    4. Der Honig ist süss.
    5. Der Stahl ist hart.   (-"-)
    6. Der Himmel ist rot.   (-"-)
    7. Der Strom ist lang.   (-"-)
    8. Das Klima ist mild.
    9. Der Winter ist kalt.   (-"-)
   10. Der Pfad ist eng.

b. The Suffix "-er"

The German suffix -er is equivalent to the English suffix -er or -or (to think - the thinker, to capture - the captor). In both languages the suffix -er forms agent nouns, i.e. nouns designating the doer of the action implied by the verb. In German, such derivatives are all masculine. Some of these nouns take an Umlaut.

b 1. From Verbs

backen	- der Bäcker	bake	- baker
handeln	- der Händler	deal	- dealer
hören	- der Hörer	listen	- listener
predigen	- der Prediger	preach	- preacher
tragen	- der Träger	carry	- carrier, porter
weben	- der Weber	weave	- weaver
einbrechen	- der Einbrecher	burglarize	- burglar
entdecken	- der Entdecker	discover	- discoverer
liebhaben	- der Liebhaber	love	- lover
Spass machen	- der Spassmacher	make fun	- joker
übersetzen	- der Übersetzer	translate	- translator
wichtig tun	- der Wichtigtuer	put on airs	- busybody

b 2. From Nouns

The suffix -er is used on nouns that denote a person's occupation:

die Burg	- der Bürger	castle, walled-in city	- citizen
das Fleisch	- der Fleischer	meat	- butcher
der Forst	- der Förster	forest	- forest ranger
das Schaf	- der Schäfer	sheep	- shepherd
die Schule	- der Schüler	school	- pupil
das Schloss	- der Schlosser	lock	- locksmith

b 3. Affixed to place names, -er denotes a person's nationality
or place of residence:

Berlin	-	der Berliner	(inhabitant of Berlin)
Hamburg	-	der Hamburger	(inhabitant of Hamburg)
England	-	der Engländer	(Englishman)
Schweiz	-	der Schweizer	(the Swiss)

Most of these derivations can also be used as adjectives:

Schweizer Käse - Swiss cheese
Kölner Wasser - Eau de Cologne

b 4. The suffix -er is also productive with impersonal nouns,
especially with names of tools or instruments:

schalten	-	der Schalter	(switch)
stecken	-	der Stecker	(plug)
zählen	-	der Zähler	(-meter, e.g. gas meter)
saugen	-	der Staubsauger	(vacuum cleaner)
tragen	-	der Hosenträger	(suspenders)
löschen	-	der Feuerlöscher	(fire-extinguisher)
sprechen	-	der Fernsprecher	(telephone)
ziehen	-	der Schraubenzieher	(screwdriver)

c. The Suffix "-in"

Many masculine nouns denoting rank, occupation, or nationality may add
the suffix -in to form the corresponding feminine nouns:

der Hamburger	-	die Hamburgerin	(woman from Hamburg)
der Engländer	-	die Engländerin	(English woman)
der Lehrer	-	die Lehrerin	(woman teacher)
der Freund	-	die Freundin	(girl friend)
der König	-	die Königin	(queen)
der Gott	-	die Göttin	(goddess)
der Löwe	-	die Löwin	(lioness)

Practice 41 :

Give the meanings of the following words.

1. arbeiten	(work)	das Arbeiten, die Arbeit, der Arbeiter, die Arbeiterin
2. besuchen	(visit)	das Besuchen, der Besuch, der Besucher, die Besucherin
3. dienen	(serve)	das Dienen, der Dienst, der Diener, die Dienerin
4. kochen	(cook)	das Kochen, der Koch, der Kocher, die Köchin
5. lehren	(teach)	das Lehren, die Lehre, der Lehrer, die Lehrerin
6. rauchen	(smoke)	das Rauchen, der Rauch, der Raucher, die Raucherin
7. schneiden	(cut)	das Schneiden, der Schnitt, der Schneider, die Schneiderin
8. tanzen	(dance)	das Tanzen, der Tanz, der Tänzer, die Tänzerin
9. verkaufen	(sell)	das Verkaufen, der Verkauf, der Verkäufer, die Verkäuferin
10. wählen	(vote, elect)	das Wählen, die Wahl, der Wähler

Practice 42 :

In accordance with the model, complete the sentences with a compound noun.

Model: Wer Fussball spielt, ist ein Fussballspieler. (soccer player)
      Wer einen Rat gibt, ist ein Ratgeber. (counselor)

   1. Wer radfährt, ist ein . . . . .   (cyclist) ; stem"-a"
   2. Wer skiläuft, ist ein . . . . .   (skier)
   3. Wer nichts tut, ist ein . . . . .   (a do-nothing); stem "-tu-"
   4. Wer nicht raucht, ist ein . . . . .   (non-smoker)
   5. Wer Kleider macht, ist ein . . . . .   (tailor)
   6. Wer Bücher druckt, ist ein . . . . .   (printer) ; use singular!
   7. Wer Uhren macht, ist ein . . . . .   (watchmaker) ; use singular!
   8. Wer Fenster putzt, ist ein . . . . .   (window cleaner)
   9. Wer Landschaften malt, ist ein . . .   (landscape-painter) ; use conn. -s!
  10. Wer eine Ehe bricht, ist ein . . . .   (adulterer); stem "-e"
  11. Wer lange schläft, ist ein . . . . .   (a late sleeper);drop -e!
  12. Wer Arbeit gibt, ist ein . . . . .   (employer); stem "-e-"

Practice 43 :

In accordance with the model, form sentences.

Model: Ein Maler übt sich im Malen.   (painting)
      Ein Boxer übt sich im Boxen.   (boxing)

   1. Ein Zeichner . . . . .   (drawing)
   2. Ein Flieger . . . . .   (flying)
   3. Ein Leser . . . . . .   (reading)
   4. Ein Schwimmer . . . . .   (swimming)
   5. Ein Segler . . . . .   (sailing); an "-e" is inserted after "-g"
   6. Ein Ruderer . . . . .   (rowing)
   7. Ein Sänger . . . . .   (singing);use infinitive -stem !
   8. Ein Läufer . . . . .   (running); use infinitive -stem !
   9. Ein Reiter . . . . .   (horseback riding)
  10. Ein Jäger . . . . . .   (hunting); drop the umlaut!

   d. Suffixes "-ler" and "-ner"

These suffixes correspond in their functions to the suffix -er, but are not
as extensively used as this one. The basis is normally a noun.

die Pforte	- der Pförtner	gate, door	- doorman
die Rede	- der Redner	speech	- speaker
die Rente	- der Rentner	pension	- pensioner
die Schuld	- der Schuldner	debt	- debtor
der Sold	- der Söldner	pay	- mercenary
das Dorf	- der Dörfler	village	- villager
die Kunst	- der Künstler	art	- artist
der Sport	- der Sportler	sport	- sportsman
der Ausflug	- der Ausflügler	excursion	- excursionist
die Volkskunde	- der Volkskundler	folklore	- folklorist

e. The Suffix "-ling"

-ling is affixed to adjectives, nouns and verbs in order to form masculine nouns designating persons. The notion of derogation is sometimes associated with such nouns.

e 1. From Adjectives (often expressing negative qualities)

fremd	- der Fremdling	strange	- stranger
jung	- der Jüngling	young	- young man, youth
feig	- der Feigling	cowardly	- coward
roh	- der Rohling	rude, brutal	- brute, ruffian
schwach	- der Schwächling	weak	- weakling

e 2. From Nouns

der Hof	- der Höfling	court	- courtier
die Flucht	- der Flüchtling	flight	- refugee
die Gunst	- der Günstling	favor	- favorite
der Dichter	- der Dichterling	poet	- poor poet
der Schreiber	- der Schreiberling	writer	- poor writer

e 3. From Verbs

lehren	- der Lehrling	teach	- apprentice
mischen	- der Mischling	mix	- half-breed
prüfen	- der Prüfling	examine	- examinee
schützen	- der Schützling	protect	- protégé
strafen	- der Sträfling	penalize	- convict

f. The Suffix "-el"

-el , a rather inactive suffix, is chiefly employed with names of tools.

decken	- der Deckel	cover	- cover, lid
heben	- der Hebel	lift, raise	- lever
klingen	- die Klingel	sound	- doorbell
schlagen	- der Schlägel	strike	- mallet
stechen	- der Stachel	sting, prick	- sting, prick

Practice 44 :

For each of the underlined words in the following sentences give a related noun ending in one of the suffixes indicated. Umlaut and other necessary changes in the stem are shown.

Nouns ending in -ler :

1. Er isst Rohkost (vegetarian diet). Er ist ein . . . . . . (ü).
2. Er kommt aus dem Erzgebirge (name of a mountain range). Er ist ein . . . . .
3. Er dient der Wissenschaft (science). Er ist ein . . . . . .

4. Er ist auf <u>Sommerfrisch</u>(e)(summer resort). Er ist ein . . . .
5. Er ist im <u>Zuchthaus</u> (penitentiary). Er ist ein . . . . . (ᵘ)
6. Er ist ein Experte in <u>Arbeitsrecht</u> (labor law). Er ist ein . . . . . .

Nouns ending in -ner :

1. Er arbeitet im <u>Gart</u>(en). Er ist ein . . . .(ᵘ)
2. Er läutet die <u>Glock</u>(en). Er ist ein . . . .(ᵘ)
3. Er spielt die <u>Harf</u>(e). Er ist ein . . . . . .
4. Er macht <u>Bühnenbild</u>(er) (stage scenery). Er ist ein . . . . .
5. Er <u>lügt</u>(to lie). Er ist ein . . . .

Nouns ending in -ling :

1. Das Kind wird (ge)<u>tauf</u>(t) (baptize). Es ist ein . . . . (ᵘ)
2. Das Kind wird (ge)<u>fund</u>(en). Es ist ein . . . . . . (stem "find").
3. Das Kind <u>kommt nach</u>. Es ist ein . . . . . (ᵘ)
4. Das Kind wird (er)<u>zog</u>(en). Es ist ein . . . . . (ᵘ)
5. Das Kind wird (ge)<u>pflegt</u> (take care of, nurse). Es ist ein . . . . .
6. Das Kind ist sehr <u>frech</u> (fresh, insolent). Es ist ein . . . . . .

g. The Suffixes "-chen" and "-lein"

They are added to nouns to form diminutives. Compare English "booklet",
"doggie" , etc. Sometimes the resulting nouns express affection or
endearment rather than smallness. All diminutive forms are neuter and
add an Umlaut, if possible. Nouns with a final -e drop this ending.

die Kirche	- das Kirchlein	(little church)
das Haus	- das Häuschen	(little house)
das Buch	- das Büchlein	(booklet)
die Mutter	- das Mütterlein	(dear mother)
Hans	- Hänschen	(dear little John)

Note:

das Brötchen	the roll
das Fräulein	young lady, Miss
das Mädchen	the girl

h. The Suffix "-ei" ("-erei")

h 1. The suffix -ei is affixed to agent nouns to denote a trade or the
place where this trade is practiced. All words ending in -ei are
feminine. The word stress is on the suffix. (Compare the French suffix
-ie in "boucherie" - butcher shop).

der Abt	- die Abtei	abbot	-	abbey
der Bäcker	- die Bäckerei	baker	-	bakery
der Konditor	- die Konditorei	confectioner	-	pastry shop
der Melker	- die Molkerei	milker	-	dairy
der Töpfer	- die Töpferei	potter	-	pottery
der Wäscher	- die Wäscherei	laundryman	-	laundry

h 2. Nouns ending in -erei indicate frequent action, often in a
    derogatory sense:

der Dieb	- die Dieberei	thief	- thievery
die Frage	- die Fragerei	question	- annoying questioning
das Kind	- die Kinderei	child	- childish trick
die Rede	- die Rederei	talk	- a lot of talking
das Spiel	- die Spielerei	play	- useless play or pastime
das Schwein	- die Schweinerei	pig	- mess, filthiness

Practice 45 :

Give the place of activity in the following sentences.

1. Der Brauer arbeitet in der . . . . . . (brewery).
2. Der Drucker arbeitet in der . . . . . . (print-shop).
3. Der Fleischer arbeitet in der . . . . . (butcher shop).
4. Der Förster arbeitet in der . . . . . . (forester's house).
5. Der Gärtner arbeitet in der . . . . . . (nursery).
6. Der Schlosser arbeitet in der . . . . . (locksmith's workshop).
7. Der Schneider arbeitet in der . . . . . (tailor shop).
8. Der Schreiner arbeitet in der . . . . . (cabinetmaker's workshop).
9. Der Spinner arbeitet in der . . . . . . (spinning-mill).
10. Der Weber arbeitet in der . . . . . . (weaving-mill).

Practice 46 :

State the English equivalents of the following nouns.

1. Fresserei
2. Kriecherei
3. Leserei
4. Plauderei
5. Prahlerei
6. Schlägerei
7. Schiesserei
8. Zauberei

i. The Suffixes "-heit", "-igkeit", and "-keit"

i 1. The suffix -heit, often equivalent to English -hood, is employed
     mainly with adjectives and participles to form abstract nouns:

dumm	- die Dummheit	stupid, dumb	- stupidity
einfach	- die Einfachheit	simple	- simplicity
gleich	- die Gleichheit	equal, same	- equality
falsch	- die Falschheit	false	- falsehood
sicher	- die Sicherheit	certain, sure	- certainty
zufrieden	- die Zufriedenheit	satisfied	- satisfaction
nachtblind	- die Nachtblindheit	night-blind	- night-blindness
entschlossen	- **die Entschlossen-**	**determined**	- **determination**
	heit		
berühmt	- die Berühmtheit	famous	- renown, **fame**
verdorben	- die Verdorbenheit	corrupt	- corruptness

Derivatives with a substantival base are very rare:

die Christen	-	die Christenheit	Christians	- Christianity
das Kind	-	die Kindheit	child	- childhood
der Narr	-	die Narrheit	fool	- folly
der Mensch	-	die Menschheit	man	- mankind

i 2. The suffix -keit which corresponds in its function to -heit is
     used in combination with adjectives ending in -ig, -lich, -bar
     and -sam. (-keit is etymologically -ig + -heit).

richtig	-	die Richtigkeit	correct	- correctness
schwierig	-	die Schwierigkeit	difficult	- difficulty
traurig	-	die Traurigkeit	sad	- sadness
deutlich	-	die Deutlichkeit	distinct	- distinctness
freundlich	-	die Freundlichkeit	friendly	- friendliness
wirklich	-	die Wirklichkeit	real	- reality
essbar	-	die Essbarkeit	edible	- edibility
fruchtbar	-	die Fruchtbarkeit	fertile	- fertility
kostbar	-	die Kostbarkeit	**precious**	- **preciousness**
einsam	-	die Einsamkeit	lonely	- loneliness
genügsam	-	die Genügsamkeit	frugal	- frugality
wachsam	-	die Wachsamkeit	vigilant	- vigilance

i 3. Certain adjectives may use the suffix -igkeit:

genau	-	die Genauigkeit	exact	- exactness
gerecht	-	die Gerechtigkeit	just	- justice
lebhaft	-	die Lebhaftigkeit	lively	- liveliness
leicht	-	die Leichtigkeit	easy, light	- ease, lightness
schnell	-	die Schnelligkeit	fast, speedy	- speed
schlaflos	-	die Schlaflosig-		
		keit	sleepless	- sleeplessness, insomnia

All nouns so derived are feminine.

Practice 47 :

In accordance with the model, form nouns from adjectives and make the necessary
adjustments in the sentences.

Model: Das Land ist frei (free).   - die Freiheit des Landes (freedom)
       Der Mensch ist kühn (bold).   - die Kühnheit des Menschen (boldness)

a.)   Nouns ending in -heit:

   1. Die Frau ist schön (pretty).
   2. Das Kind ist krank (sick).
   3. Die Nacht ist dunkel (dark).
   4. Der Junge ist frech (fresh).
   5. Der Diamant ist echt (genuine).
   6. Der Dichter ist beliebt (popular).
   7. Der Tod ist gewiss (certain).
   8. Der Sommer ist trocken (dry).
   9. Das Tier ist klug (clever).
  10. Die Geschichte ist wahr (true).

b.)   Nouns ending in -keit:

1. Der Verkehr ist gefährlich (dangerous).
2. Gott ist ewig (eternal).
3. Das Wetter ist veränderlich (changeable).
4. Der Soldat ist tapfer (brave).
5. Der Professor ist vergesslich (forgetful).
6. Der Tempel ist heilig (sacred).
7. Die Wohnung ist sauber (clean).
8. Die Forschung ist wichtig (important).
9. Die Sekretärin ist tüchtig (efficient).
10. Die Bewohner sind höflich (polite).

j. The Suffix "-nis"

The suffix -nis, by which we form an abstract noun from an adjective or a verb stem, corresponds in function to English -ness. Nouns with -nis are either feminine or neuter.

j 1. Nouns formed from adjectives indicate a condition or quality:

bitter	-	die Bitternis	bitter	- bitterness
faul	-	die Fäulnis	rotten	- rottenness
finster	-	die Finsternis	dark	- darkness
geheim	-	das Geheimnis	secret	- the secret
gleich	-	das Gleichnis	similar	- simile, parable
wild	-	die Wildnis	wild	- wilderness

j 2. Nouns formed from verb stems (especially such as have prefixes) indicate an act, activity or the result of the activity:

begraben	-	das Begräbnis	bury	- burial
erlauben	-	die Erlaubnis	permit	- permission
fangen	-	das Gefängnis	catch	- prison, jail
kennen	-	die Erkenntnis	know	- knowledge, insight
erzeugen	-	das Erzeugnis	produce	- product
verzeichnen	-	das Verzeichnis	list, register	- index, register

Practice 48 :

In accordance with the model, form nouns with -nis and give the English meaning.

Model: Was ärgert (to make angry), ist ein Ärgernis (scandal, offence).
       Was betrübt (to afflict), ist ein Betrübnis (affliction, grief).

1. Was hemmt (obstruct), ist ein . . . . . .
2. Was hindert (hinder), ist ein . . . . . .
3. Was sich ereignet (occur), ist ein . . . .
4. Was sich ergibt (result from), ist ein . . . . . . (stem -e)
5. Was erlebt wird (experience), ist ein . . . . .
6. Was erzeugt wird (produce), ist ein . . . .
7. Was gelobt wird (vow), ist ein . . . . (Umlaut)
8. Was gestanden wird (confess), ist ein . . . . . . (Umlaut)
9. Was vermacht wird (bequeath), ist ein . . . . . . (Umlaut -tnis)
10. Was versäumt wird (omit), ist ein . . . .

k. The Suffixes "-sal" and "-sel"

-sal and -sel are not very productive suffixes. They are usually found after verbal stems and always form neuter nouns.

-sal

laben	- das Labsal	refresh	- refreshment
rinnen	- das Rinnsal	flow, run	- watercourse
scheuen	- das Scheusal	fear	- monster
schicken	- das Schicksal	send	- fate (that which is sent)
verwirren	- das Wirrsal	confuse	- chaos

-sel often denotes something insignificant or contemptible:

anhängen	- das Anhängsel	hang on	- pendant, tag
füllen	- das Füllsel	fill	- stuffing
mitbringen	- das Mitbringsel	bring along	- little present
schreiben	- das Geschreibsel	write	- scribbling
überbleiben	- das Überbleibsel	be left	- leftovers

l. The Suffix "-schaft"

-schaft, often equivalent to English -ship as in friendship, is most frequently attached to nouns to derive abstract nouns and collectives (groups of people). These nouns are always feminine.

l 1. Abstract Nouns

der Freund	- die Freundschaft	friend	- friendship
der Herr	- die Herrschaft	master	- rule, dominion
der Kamerad	- die Kameradschaft	comrade	- comradeship
die Mutter	- die Mutterschaft	mother	- maternity
der Ritter	- die Ritterschaft	knight	- knighthood
der Staats-bürger	- die Staatsbürger-schaft	citizen	- citizenship

l 2. Collectives

der Arbeiter	- die Arbeiterschaft	worker	- working class
der Beamte	- die Beamtenschaft	civil servant	- civil servants
der Bruder	- die Bruderschaft	brother	- fraternity
der Geselle	- die Gesellschaft	companion	- society
der Verwandte	- die Verwandtschaft	relative	- relatives

"meine Herrschaften" (direct address) ladies and gentlemen !

l 3. Derivatives with Verbal Base

erringen	- die Errungenschaft	achieve	- achievement
fangen	- die Gefangenschaft	capture	- captivity
wandern	- die Wanderschaft	wander	- wandering, traveling
wissen	- die Wissenschaft	know	- science

Practice 49 :

Form collectives in accordance with the model.

Model: alle Ärzte   (all the physicians)   - die Ärzteschaft
       alle Einwohner(all the inhabitants)   - die Einwohnerschaft

   1. alle Bürger   (all the citizens)
   2. alle Diener   (all the servants)
   3. alle Bauern   (all the farmers)
   4. alle Kollegen (all the colleagues)
   5. alle Mitglied(er) (all the members)
   6. alle Nachbar(n) (all the neighbors)
   7. alle Lehrer   (all the teachers)
   8. alle Studenten (all the students)
   9. alle Nachkommen (all the descendants)
  10. alle Priester (all the priests)

   m. The Suffix "-tum"

-tum is cognate with English -dom as in king<u>dom</u> . Most derivatives have
a substantival base, but the suffix may also be affixed to adjectives and
verbs. -tum, -schaft, and -heit have approximately the same force when
attached to the same stem. See table on page 61.

der Besitz	- das Besitztum	possession	- property, possession
der Bürger	- das Bürgertum	citizen	- middle class
der Christ	- das Christentum	Christian	- Christianity
der Priester	- das Priestertum	priest	- priesthood
der Ritter	- das Rittertum	knight	- chivalry
das Volk	- das Volkstum	nation	- nationality
reich	- der Reichtum	rich	- richness, wealth
eigen	- das Eigentum	own	- property
irren	- der Irrtum	err	- error
wachsen	- das Wachstum	grow	- growth

   n. The Suffix "-ung"

Among the most productive native suffixes for the formation of nouns from
verbs is -ung , cognate with English -ing . The nouns so derived are all
feminine. They indicate the action or the result of the action of the verb.

bewundern	- die Bewunderung	admire	- admiration
erfinden	- die Erfindung	invent	- invention
verschwenden	- die Verschwendung	waste	- the waste
einladen	- die Einladung	invite	- invitation
aufführen	- die Aufführung	perform	- performance
übersetzen	- die Übersetzung	translate	- translation
unterhalten	- die Unterhaltung	entertain	- entertainment
möblieren	- die Möblierung	furnish	- furnishing
führen	- die Führung	guide	- guidance
meinen	- die Meinung	think,mean	- meaning

Few derivatives denote concrete things:

kleiden	- die Kleidung	clothe, dress-	**clothing**
erfrischen	- die Erfrischung	refresh	- refreshment
wohnen	- die Wohnung	live, **reside**	- apartment
zeichnen	- die Zeichnung	draw	- drawing

Practice 50 :

Form feminine nouns in -ung and give their meanings.

1. bedeuten (mean)
2. hand(e)ln (act)
3. erziehen (educate)
4. regieren (govern)
5. erfahren (experience)
6. reinigen (clean)
7. vorlesen (lecture)
8. beschäftigen (**employ**)
9. retten (save)
10. verbinden (connect)
11. üben (practice)
12. achten (respect)

Practice 51 :

In the following sentences express the nouns with -ung verbally and make the necessary changes.

Model: Die Versammlung der Studenten fand in der Aula statt.
Die Studenten versammelten sich in der Aula.

1. Edison machte die Erfindung des Grammophons. 2. Columbus machte die Entdeckung Amerikas. 3. Der Regen war für uns eine angenehme Erfrischung. 4. Die Heilung der Wunde ging nur sehr langsam vor sich. 5. Er hatte zur Unterhaltung der Gäste das Radio angestellt. 6. Die Fütterung der Tiere ist verboten. 7. Tragen Sie warme Kleidung, sonst werden Sie sich eine Erkältung holen. 8. Die Erziehung der Kinder ist heutzutage sehr schwer. 9. Die Begegnung der beiden Männer fand gestern statt (reflexive). 10. Wir müssen zu einer Entscheidung kommen.

o. Formation of Collective Nouns

We turn finally to the formation of collectives and similar substantives by means other than suffixes alone. Here we must mention the use of Ge- as a collective noun-prefix. In many cases nouns so derived also take an -e ending, or they make changes in the stem vowel. They are with very few exceptions neuter.

o 1. The Prefix Ge- (with or without an -e ending)

der Berg	- das Gebirge	mountain	- mountain range
der Busch	- das Gebüsch	bush	- shrubbery, bushes

das Horn	-	das Gehörn	horn	-	horns, antlers
der Stein	-	das Gestein	rock	-	rocks
das Wasser	-	das Gewässer	water	-	**body of water**
die Wolke	-	das Gewölk	cloud	-	clouds

beissen	-	das Gebiss	bite	-	set of teeth, dentures
hören	-	das Gehör	hear	-	hearing
backen	-	das Gebäck	bake	-	pastry
rauschen	-	das Geräusch	rustle, roar	-	noise
schmecken	-	der Geschmack	taste	-	taste, flavor
sprechen	-	das Gespräch	speak	-	conversation

A great number of formations with <u>Ge-</u> have a certain derogatory quality:

fragen	-	das Gefrage (Fragerei)	ask	-	continual questions
reden	-	das Gerede (Rederei)	talk	-	gossip, rumor
schmieren	-	das Geschmiere	smear	-	scribbling, scrawl
singen	-	das Gesinge	sing	-	poor singing
tun	-	das Getue	do, act	-	fuss
das Hinundhergelaufe (Lauferei)			unpleasant running about		

Practice 52 :

For each of the following words give a related noun with <u>Ge-</u> , and its English meaning. The need for vowel change and <u>-e</u> ending is indicated.

die Feder	(feather)	(-ie-)	
das Holz	(wood)	(-"-)	
die Mauer	(wall)	(-"-)	
der Flügel	(wing)		
das Recht	(law)	(-i)	
der Strauch	(bush, shrub)	(-"-)	
brüllen	(roar, yell)		
folgen	(follow)	(- + -e)	
fühlen	(feel)		
riechen	(smell)	(-u-)	(masculine)
schenken	(give)		
packen	(pack)	(-"-)	
wachsen	(grow)	(-"-)	

o 2. <u>Independent Nouns Used as Suffixes</u>

Many German suffixes were once independent words. Through frequent use their original sense has been lost. This process is still active today with words like <u>Gut</u>, <u>Werk</u>, <u>Wesen</u>, and <u>Zeug</u>, to name a few examples. As nouns they have their own meanings, but when attached to other substantives, they act as collective suffixes indicating the notion of belonging to a group of individuals or objects, or expressing other collective ideas.

"-gut" (literal meaning: "goods")

der Dieb	- das Dieb(e)sgut	thief	- stolen goods
der Gedanke	- das Gedankengut	thought	- ideas
das Lied	- das Liedgut	song	- songs
der Stein	- das Steingut	stone, rock	- stoneware, crockery
der Strand	- das Strandgut	beach	- **things washed ashore**
mahlen	- das Mahlgut	grind	- grain

"-werk" (literal meanings: "work", "works", "deed", "production")

der Busch	- das Buschwerk(Gebüsch)	bush	- shrubbery
die Schrift	- das Schriftwerk (Schrifttum)	writing	- literature
der Zucker	- das Zuckerwerk (or -ware)	sugar	- candy
backen	- das Backwerk (Gebäck)	bake	- pastry
schnitzen	- das Schnitzwerk	carve	- carving
treiben	- das Triebwerk	drive	- gearing

"-wesen" (literal meanings: "nature", "manners", "concern", "system")

die Fürsorge	- das Fürsorgewesen	welfare	- social welfare (system)
das Geld	- das Geldwesen	money	- money affairs
der Flug	- das Flugwesen	flight	- aviation
das Gericht	- das Gerichtswesen	law court	- judiciary
die Schule	- das Schulwesen	school	- school affairs, education
werben	- das Werbewesen	advertise	- advertising

"-zeug" (literal meanings: "stuff", "things", "tool", "utensil", "machine")

das Bett	- das Bettzeug	bed	- linen
grün	- das Grünzeug	green	- greens
fahren	- das Fahrzeug	drive, ride	- vehicle
nähen	- das Nähzeug	sew	- sewing kit
rasieren	- das Rasierzeug	shave	- shaving **kit**
spielen	- das Spielzeug	play	- toy

Practice 53 :

Give the English meanings of the following collective nouns:

das Beutegut (Beute - booty)	das Buschwerk
das Erzählgut	das Laubwerk (Laub - leaves)
das Geistesgut	das Mauerwerk
das Wissensgut	das **Tauwerk**

das Bildungswesen das Feuerzeug
das Eisenbahnwesen das Schreibzeug
das Filmwesen das Schuhzeug
das Gesundheitswesen das Schulzeug

p. Survey of Noun Suffixes

For the purpose of review, all German noun suffixes are divided into groups according to the sort of formative power they exercise in the process of word-making.

Names of persons associated with a certain place, profession **or** activity	-er: Leser, Bäcker, Lehrer, Berliner, Vierziger -ler: Wissenschaftler, Sportler, Sommerfrischler -ner: Pförtner, Rentner, Schuldner, Redner -ling: Fremdling, Lehrling, Feigling, Fünfling
Names of tools **or** instruments	-er: Kocher, Schalter, Plattenspieler, Stecker -el: Hebel, Deckel, Klingel, Schlägel, Stachel -zeug: Rasierzeug, Spielzeug, Fahrzeug
Names of places	-e: Schmiede, Viehweide, Schwemme (watering place) -ei: Gärtnerei, Bücherei, Fleischerei, Bäckerei
Names of concrete things	-e: Grube, Fuhre, Stiege, Speise, Pfeife, Feile -nis: Erzeugnis, Verzeichnis, Hindernis -sel: Mitbringsel, Anhängsel, Füllsel -ung: Kleidung, Wohnung, Ladung, Zeichnung, Bindung -werk: Schnitzwerk, Backwerk, Zuckerwerk
Collectives	-heit: Menschheit, Christenheit, Kindheit -schaft: Lehrerschaft, Arbeiterschaft, Gesellschaft -tum: Bürgertum, Rittertum, Priestertum -gut: Liedgut, Gedankengut, Diebsgut -werk: Buschwerk, Schriftwerk, Triebwerk -wesen: Schulwesen, Geldwesen, Flugwesen -zeug: Bettzeug, Grünzeug, Schlagzeug Ge-(-e): Gebirge, Gewässer, Gestein, Gebüsch
Nouns denoting activity, result of activity **or** condition	-e: Lage, Hilfe, Übergabe, Suche, Reise -ei: Lauferei, Spielerei, Rederei, Fragerei -nis: Begräbnis, Erlebnis, Wagnis -schaft: Feindschaft, Freundschaft, Mutterschaft -tum: Irrtum, Wachstum, Reichtum -ung: Verschwendung, Erfindung, Einladung Ge-(-e): Gefrage, Gerede, Getue, Gelaufe

Nouns denoting a characteristic	-e: Grösse, Höhe, Stärke, Kürze
	-heit: Sicherheit, Dummheit, Falschheit
	-keit: Wirklichkeit, Einsamkeit, Richtigkeit
	-igkeit:Genauigkeit, Leichtigkeit, Schnelligkeit

5. Formation of Adjectives and Adverbs by Means of Suffixes

Adjectival suffixes form adjectives, most of which, in their uninflected form, may be used adverbially. Here, too, we often find correspondence between English and Germanic suffixes. Compare:

day	- daily	Tag	- täglich
thirst	- thirsty	Durst	- durstig
child	- childish	Kind	- kindisch
wool	- woolen	Wolle	- wollen

However, the student will encounter a great many German adjectives whose English equivalents are not produced in the German way, but are rather drawn from a different root, mainly from Latin. The English counterpart for the German adjective "mündlich", which is derived from "der Mund" (mouth), is not "mouthy" but "oral". Likewise "Haus" (house) gives us "häuslich", but "domestic" in English. There are hundreds of similar cases. At any rate, the German adjectives should be immediately recognizable, provided the student is familiar with the German base word.

a. The Suffix "bar"

-bar, once an independent adjective meaning bearing, producing, is often equivalent to English -ible and -able. Most adjectives with -bar have a passive meaning, e.g. Die Frucht ist essbar (edible) - Sie kann gegessen werden.
- Sie lässt sich essen.

der Dank	- dankbar	thank	- thankful
die Frucht	- fruchtbar	fruit	- fertile, fruitful
die Furcht	- furchtbar	fear	- terrible, fearful
die Sicht	- sichtbar	sight	- visible
das Schiff	- schiffbar	ship	- navigable
denken	- denkbar	think, imagine	- thinkable, imaginable
erreichen	- erreichbar	reach, attain	- attainable
fahren	- fahrbar	drive	- movable
greifen	- greifbar	seize, touch	- seizable, tangible
strafen	- strafbar	punish	- punishable
zahlen	- zahlbar	pay	- payable

Practice 54 :

In accordance with the model, form adjectives with -bar from the verbs below, and give the English meanings.

Model: Die Frucht lässt sich essen. Sie ist essbar (edible).
       Die Krankheit kann geheilt werden. Sie ist heilbar (curable).

1. Die Aufgabe lässt sich lösen.
2. Dir Strasse lässt sich befahren.
3. Der Fortschritt kann gesehen werden. (stem   sicht-)
4. Das Schloss lässt sich bewohnen.
5. Die Maschine kann gebraucht werden.
6. Der Ton kann gehört werden.
7. Das Wasser lässt sich trinken.
8. Die Zahl lässt sich teilen.
9. Das Kleid kann gewaschen werden.
10. Das kann nicht definiert werden.
11. Der Apparat lässt sich tragen.
12. Der Weg kann (be)gangen werden.

b. The Suffixes "-en" and "-ern"

-en and -ern, corresponding to English -en and -ern, are affixed to nouns
indicating a material.

das Gold	- golden	gold	- golden, made of gold
die Erde	- irden	earth	- earthen, made of clay
das Blei	- bleiern	lead	- leaden, made of lead
das Holz	- hölzern	wood	- wooden, made of wood
das Leder	- ledern	leather	- leathern, made of leather
die Seide	- seiden	silk	- silken, made of silk

Practice 55 :

Replace the adjectives with expressions as indicated in the model.

Model: ein seidenes Kleid (silk) - ein Kleid aus Seide - ein Seidenkleid

1. eine gläserne Tür   (glass)
2. ein wollenes Tuch   (wool)
3. ein silberner Löffel   (silver)
4. ein samtener Hut   (velvet)
5. ein eisernes Gitter   (iron)
6. ein kupferner Kessel   (copper)
7. ein papierenes Tischtuch   (paper)
8. ein eichener Tisch   (oak)

c. The Suffix "-er"

There is a small group of adverbs denoting a position in space. From these
adverbs we can form adjectives by adding -er to the stem.

oben	- ober-	on top, upstairs, above	- upper
unten	- unter-	at the bottom, downstairs, below	- lower
aussen	- äusser-	outside	- outer, external

innen	- inner-	inside	- inner, internal
mitten	- mittler-	in the middle	- middle, medium
vorne	- vorder-	in front	- front
hinten	- hinter-	in the back	- back, hind

d. The Suffix "-haft"

This suffix is usually added to nouns and verb stems to form adjectives with the general **meaning** of "having the quality (nature) of", e.g. "mannhaft" (manlike) having the quality of a man.

der Geschmack-	schmackhaft	taste	- palatable, relishable
die Scham	- schamhaft	shame	- shamefaced, bashful
die Sünde	- sündhaft	sin	- sinful
die Tugend	- tugendhaft	virtue	- virtuous

Certain nouns take the connective -en between the stem and the suffix:

die Frau	- frauenhaft	woman	- womanlike
der Greis	- greisenhaft	old man	- senile
der Held	- heldenhaft	hero	- heroic
der Riese	- riesenhaft	giant	- gigantic

glauben	- glaubhaft	believe	- credible, trustworthy
lehren	- lehrhaft	teach	- instructive, didactic
schmeicheln	- schmeichelhaft	flatter	- flattering
wohnen	- wohnhaft	live	- resident, living

-haft is rarely attached to adjectives:

krankhaft	morbid
wahrhaft	truthful

Practice 56 :

In accordance with the model, form adjectives with -haft from the nouns and verbs in the following sentences.

Model: Das, was Fehler (defect, flaw) hat, ist fehlerhaft (defective).

1. Das, was dauert (last), ist . . . . .
2. Das, was einen Vorteil (profit) bringt, ist . . . . .
3. Das, was schmerzt (hurt), ist . . . .
4. Das, was einen Schaden (damage) hat, ist . . . . .
5. Das, was wie ein Traum (dream) ist, ist . . . . . .
6. Ein Mensch, der gern nascht (have a sweet tooth), ist . . . . . .
7. Ein Kind, das gern schwatzt (talk **idly,chatter**), **ist** . . . . .
8. Ein Kind, das sich sehr schämt (be ashamed), ist . . . . .
9. Ein Mensch, der Laster (vices) hat, ist . . . . .
10. Ein Mensch, dem man glauben (trust) kann, ist . . . . .

e. The Suffix "-ig"

-ig, the commonest adjective suffix, can be found with adjectives or adverbs
and verbs, but most often with nouns, and even with compounds. Derivatives
formed with -ig may denote the following:

e 1. Possession of the Thing Implied in the Noun

das Blut	- blutig	blood	- bloody
der Geist	- geistig	mind, intellect	- mental, intellectual
das Gespräch	- gesprächig	talk	- talkative
die Lust	- lustig	joy	- joyful
der Schmutz	- schmutzig	dirt, filth	- dirty, filthy
die Vorsicht	- vorsichtig	caution	- cautious
breite Schultern-	breitschultrig	broad shoulders -	broad-shouldered
dicker Leib	- dickleibig	bulky figure	- corpulent

e 2. Similarity

(wie) Glass	- glasig	(like)glass	- glassy
Gold	- goldig	gold	- lovely, cute
Korn	- körnig	grain	- granular
Milch	- milchig	milk	- milky
Ries(e)	- riesig	giant	- huge
Schnee	- schneeig	snow	- snowy

With certain stems -ig has much the same force as -haft , e.g.
riesig - riesenhaft.

e 3. Quality Associated with the Activity Implied in the Verb

beissen	- bissig	bite	- snappish
finden	- findig	find	- resourceful, ingenious
gefallen	- gefällig	please	- pleasing
kleben	- klebrig (-rig)	stick	- sticky
schlafen	- schläfrig(-rig)	sleep	- sleepy
schlüpfen	- schlüpfrig (-rig)	slip	- slippery

e 4. A number of rather frequent adverbs form adjectives by adding the suffix -ig.

heute	- die heutige Jugend	(today's youth)
gestern	- die gestrige Zeitung	(yesterday's paper)
hier	- die hiesige Bevölkerung	(the population here)
dort	- die dortigen Gebräuche	(the customs there)
jetzt	- die jetzige Mode	(present fashion)
bisher	- die bisherigen Versuche	(the attempts made so far)
oben	- der obige Satz	(the above sentence)

Practice 57 :

Replace the underlined expressions by adjectives with -ig , and make the
necessary changes in the sentences.

Model: Mit Mut (courage) begegneten sie der Gefahr. Mutig begegneten sie der Gefahr.
        Das Kind hat blondes Haar.(blond hair)   Es ist blondhaarig.

1. Der Student zeigt Eif(e)r und Ehrgeiz.(zeal and ambition) Er ist . . . .
2. Er hat die Begier(de) (desire) zu lernen.   Er ist . . . .
3. Wir haben Hung(e)r und Durst. (hunger and thirst)   Wir sind . . . . . .
4. Süddeutschland hat Wäld(er) und Gebirg(e). (forests and mountains) (no Umlaut)
5. Ihr Gesicht hatte schon Falt(en). (wrinkles)
6. Die Suppe hat zuviel Salz und Pfeffer. (salt and pepper)
7. Er hat die Schuld (blame) an diesem Unglück.
8. Haben Sie die Güt(e) (kindness) und nehmen Sie das zurück.
9. Die Bevölkerung von hier (here) interessiert sich nicht dafür.(stem "hies-")
10. Die Jugend von heut(e) (today) lebt anders als die Jugend von gest(e)r(n). (yesterda
11. Bitte kommen Sie zur recht(en) Zeit ! (on time)
12. Das Brot da ist wie ein Schwamm. (sponge)
13. Die alten Freunde sassen in Eintracht (harmony) beisammen. (Umlaut)
14. Wir haben alles mit Geduld und Ruh(e) (patience and calm) ertragen.
15. Der Wein schmeckt wie Wasser.(water) (Umlaut)
16. Er trägt einen Hut mit breit(em) Rand. (wide brim)
17. Dachshunde haben kurz(e) Bein(e). (short legs)
18. Das Flugzeug hat zwei Motor(en). (two engines)

f. The Suffix "-isch"

This suffix, mostly attached to nouns, often resembles the English -ish. It forms
adjectives denoting origin or type, as can be seen from the examples below.

der Dichter	- dichterisch	poet	- poetic
der Erfinder	- erfinderisch	inventor	- inventive
der Künstler	- künstlerisch	artist	- artistic
der Narr	- närrisch	fool	- foolish
der Sportsmann	- sportsmännisch	sportsman	- sportsmanlike
das Tier	- tierisch	animal	- bestial

das Heim	- heimisch	home	- homelike, homey
der Himmel	- himmlisch	heaven	- heavenly
die Hölle	- höllisch	hell	- infernal, hellish
die Laune	- launisch	mood	- moody
der Neid	- neidisch	envy	- envious
der Spott	- spöttisch	mockery	- mocking

Amerika	- amerikanisch	America	- American
Europa	- europäisch	Europe	- European
Rom	- römisch	Rome	- Roman
der Schotte	- schottisch	Scot	- Scottish, Scotch
das Ausland	- ausländisch	foreign country	- foreign
die Stadt	- städtisch	city, town	- urban

For adjectives with -isch formed from non-Germanic stems see pages 7 and 8, Chapter A/IV/3.

With names of persons the suffix -isch is sometimes shortened to -sch:

    die Luther<u>sche</u> Sprache   Luther's language
    eine Mahler<u>sche</u> Sinfonie   a Mahler symphony   or a symphony by Mahler

Practice 58 :

Form adjectives in -isch and give their English meanings.

der Held	(hero)	der Hohn	(scorn, sneer) (-"-)
der Herr	(master)	die Magie	(magic)
der Jud(e)	(Jew) (-"-)	das Paradies	(paradise)
der Mörder	(murderer)	die Partei	(party)
der Schöpfer	(creator)	die Rass(e)	(race)
der Student	(student)	die Schul(e)	(school)
der Verschwender	(spendthrift)	der Sturm	(storm) (-"-)
das Weib	(woman)	die Trop(en)	(tropics)

Practice 59 :

Which country are they from ? Find the names of the countries on the map.

Model: bayrisches Bier - Bier aus Bayern

1. westfälischer Schinken
2. französischer Wein
3. englische Wolle
4. irisches Leinen
5. norwegische Sardinen
6. ein rheinisches Mädchen
7. ein preussischer General
8. eine spanische Tänzerin
9. ein russischer Pianist
10. ein finnischer Skispringer

g. The Suffix "-lich"

-lich, cognate with English -ly as in "friendly", belongs to the most active adjective suffixes. It may be affixed to nouns, adjectives, and verb stems.

    g 1. When combined with nouns, it designates possession or characteristics of persons and things:

Gott	-	göttlich	God	- divine
der Mensch	-	menschlich	man	- human
der Feind	-	feindlich	enemy	- hostile
der Kaiser	-	kaiserlich	emperor	- imperial
der Friede	-	friedlich	peace	- peaceful
die Sache	-	sachlich	thing, matter	- real, relevant
der Herbst	-	herbstlich	autumn	- autumnal, autumn-like
der Sonntag	-	sonntäglich	Sunday	- Sunday

g 2. Affixed to adjectives, -lich may have an adverbial or a diminutive force:

falsch	-	fälschlich	false, wrong	- falsely
ganz	-	gänzlich	entire	- entirely
kurz	-	kürzlich	short	- recently, lately
neu	-	neulich	new, recent	- recently
krank	-	kränklich	sick	- sickly
rot	-	rötlich	red	- reddish
rund	-	rundlich	round	- roundish
schwach	-	schwächlich	weak	- weakly, feeble

g 3. Attached to verb stems the meaning of -lich is sometimes similar to that of -bar (See Chapter 5 a. on page 62):

(Passive Meaning)

erklären	-	erklärlich(-bar)	explain	- explicable
ertragen	-	erträglich	endure	- endurable, tolerable
verkaufen	-	verkäuflich	sell	- vendible, for sale
vernehmen	-	vernehmlich (-bar)	perceive	- perceptible, audible

(Active Meaning)

bedrohen	-	bedrohlich	threaten	- threatening
sterben	-	sterblich	die	- mortal
taugen	-	tauglich	be fit for, of use	- fit, apt, able
verderben	-	verderblich	spoil	- perishable

Note: When the base ends in -n, the connective -d or -t appears before -lich:

hoffentlich	-	hopefully
wissentlich	-	knowing(ly)
morgendlich	-	every morning
wöchentlich	-	every week, weekly

g 4. Nouns denoting time may take on adjectival or adverbial function by affixing -lich:

wöchentlich)		monatlich)	
einmal die Woche)	weekly	einmal im Monat)	monthly
jede Woche)		jeden Monat)	

Notice the difference here between -ig and -lich :

-ig means Duration	-lich means Repetition	
eine vierstündige Sitzung (a four-hour meeting)	vierstündlich or: alle vier Stunden	(every four hours)
eine zweimonatige Reise (a trip that lasts two months)	zweimonatlich or: alle zwei Monate	(every two months)
ein dreijähriges Kind (a three-year-old child)	vierteljährlich or: alle drei Monate	(quarterly, every three months)

Practice 60 :

Complete the sentences with adjectives in -lich.

1. Wir mussten ihn . . . . . (Tag) daran erinnern. (-"-)
2. Manche Arbeiter bekommen ihr Geld . . . . . . (Woche). (-"-) ent-
3. Das Radio bringt . . . . . (Stund(e) Nachrichten. (-"-)
4. . . . . . . (Nacht) Besuche sind hier nicht erlaubt. (-"-)
5. Dieses Weinglas ist leicht . . . . . (zerbrechen).
6. Ich habe in Frankfurt . . . . . (Geschäft) zu tun.
7. Seit dem Autounfall ist sie immer . . . . . (krank). (-"-)
8. Ich esse . . . . . (süss) Speisen nicht gern.
9. Ich habe . . . . . (Augenblick) keine Zeit für Sie.
10. Das . . . . . (König) Schloss von Potsdam wurde im Krieg zerstört.
11. Sie bekam die Stelle wegen ihrer . . . . . (Sprach(e) Kenntnisse.
12. Der Aufsatz ist . . . . . (Inhalt) sehr gut.
13. Ich habe . . . . . (Kunst) Blumen nicht gern. (-"-)
14. Die Waren im Schaufenster sind nicht . . . . . (verkaufen). (-"-)
15. Die ewigen Güter sind wichtiger als die . . . . . (Zeit).

Practice 61 :

Give the meanings of these words:

1. dichten, der Dichter, das Gedicht, die Dichtung, das Dichtwerk, dichterisch
2. erfinden, der Erfinder, die Erfindung, die Erfindungsgabe, erfinderisch
3. essen, das Essen, der Esser, die Esserei, essbar, die Essbarkeit
4. fragen, die Frage, der Frager, das Gefrage, fraglich, die Fraglichkeit
5. hausen, das Haus, häuslich, die Häuslichkeit, haushoch
6. kaufen, der Kauf, der Käufer, käuflich, der Kaufmann, kaufmännisch
7. landen, das Land, die Landung, ländlich, die Landschaft, das Gelände
8. malen, der Maler, die Malerin, die Malerei, malerisch, das Gemälde
9. träumen, der Traum, der Träumer, träumerisch, traumhaft, die Träumerei
10. wohnen, die Wohnung, wohnhaft, wohnlich, die Wohnlichkeit, der Wohnsitz

h. The Suffix "-sam"

-sam is related to English -some as in lonesome. It is usually attached to verb
stems and indicates a capability of performing the action implied in the verb, or
an inclination to do so.

arbeiten	- arbeitsam	work	- industrious (likes to work)
bedeuten	- bedeutsam	mean, signify	- significant
biegen	- biegsam	bend	- flexible
folgen	- folgsam	follow, obey	- obedient
schweigen	- schweigsam	be silent	- taciturn
sparen	- sparsam	save	- economical, **frugal**
streben	- strebsam	strive, aspire	- ambitious

In combination with nouns the suffix indicates that the thing implied in the noun is present:

ein furchtsamer Mensch   means   ein Mensch, der Furcht hat   or
                                   ein Mensch mit Furcht

Practice 62 :

Change the following phrases in accordance with the model.

Model: Ein Mensch, der Furcht hat - ein furchtsamer Mensch   (timorous)

ein Mensch, der den Fried(en) liebt   -   (peaceful)
ein Mensch mit strengen Sitt(en)   -   (modest, decent)
ein Mensch von Ehr(e)   -   (respectable)
ein Mensch, der Sorg(e) zeigt   -   (careful)
ein Mensch, der sich enthalt(en) kann   -   (abstinent)
ein Mensch, der sich füg(t)   -   (pliant)
eine Arbeit voller Mühe(e)   -   (laborious)
ein Urlaub voller Erhol(ung)   -   (recreative)
ein Tod durch Gewalt   -   (violent)

i. Adjectives Used as Suffixes

Through frequent use in word combinations certain adjectives have become suffixes.

-artig   derived from the noun "die Art", designates kind, manner, resemblance.

ein gutartiges Kind (=gute Art)   -   a good-natured child
ein turmartiges Gebäude   -   a tower-like structure

-arm   means "having little of", "being devoid of".

eine blutarme Frau   -   an anaemic woman
ein gemütsarmer Mensch   -   a man devoid of feeling

-fach   or   -fältig corresponds to English -fold.

vielfache Pflichten   -   manifold duties
vielfältige Interessen   -   various (manifold) interests
die dreifache Anzahl   -   three times the number

-frei, -leer, and -los denote lack of something (comparable to English -less, free from).

ein zollfreier Hafen   -   a duty-free port
eine lärmfreie Strasse   -   a noiseless street
der luftleere Raum   -   the vacuum
ein endloses Gerede   -   an endless talk
eine hoffnungslose Situation   -   a hopeless situation

-reich and -voll, opposites of -los, -frei, and -leer indicate fullness and richness.

eine kurvenreiche Strasse	- a winding road
eine einflussreiche Person	- an influential person
eine liebevolle Art	- an affectionate way
ein dornenvoller (dorniger) Weg	- a thorny path

-mässig meaning with regard to , as for , as to ; combinations with -mässig are especially popular, but are not always considered good German.

Er ist ihm intelligenzmässig überlegen.	- He is superior to him as far as
(Better German: Er ist ihm an Intelligenz	intelligence goes.
überlegen).	
quantitätsmässig	- quantitative

-mässig may also be equivalent to the suffix -artig.

ein kindermässiges Benehmen	- a childlike behavior
ein heldenmässiger Tod	- a heroic death

Practice 63 :

Give the English for the second word in each German word pair.

1. ausdrucksvoll	(expressive)	-	ausdruckslos	(. . . . .)
2. gefahrvoll	(perilous, dangerous)	-	gefahrlos	
3. gefühlvoll	(sentimental)	-	gefühllos	
4. geräuschvoll	(noisy)	-	geräuschlos	
5. kraftvoll	(powerful)	-	kraftlos	
6. rücksichtsvoll	(considerate)	-	rücksichtslos	
7. wertvoll	(valuable, precious)	-	wertlos	
8. gewürzreich	(spicy)	-	gewürzfrei	
9. hilfreich	(helpful)	-	hilflos	
10. kinderreich	(prolific)	-	kinderlos	
11. wasserreich	(abounding in water)	-	wasserarm	
12. fehlerhaft	(faulty, defective)	-	fehlerlos	
13. staubig	(dusty)	-	staubfrei	
14. zweckmässig	(useful)	-	zwecklos	

j.Summary of Adjective Suffixes

For the purpose of review a list of related German adjective suffixes is given in the table below. It is understood that certain suffixes with the same force cannot always be used interchangeably. Some stems prefer one suffix, some another.

Suffix	Synonymous with:	
-bar	-lich	erklärbar - erklärlich; strafbar - sträflich
-haft	-artig	zwerghaft - zwergartig (dwarfish)

-haft	-ig	riesenhaft - riesig; sündhaft - sündig
	-lich	schmerzhaft - schmerzlich; ernsthaft - ernstlich
	-mässig	heldenhaft - heldenmässig; schülerhaft - schülermässig
	-voll	zweckhaft - zweckvoll; schmerzhaft - schmerzvoll
-ig	-artig	breiig - breiartig (pulpy)
	-förmig	glockig - glockenförmig (bell-shaped)
	-lich	mitternächtig - mitternächtlich
	-reich	felsig - felsenreich (rocky)
	-voll	kräftig - kraftvoll; dornig - dornenvoll
-los	-frei	fehlerlos - fehlerfrei; sorgenlos - sorgenfrei
	-leer	wasserlos - wasserleer

Notice that certain suffixes sometimes touch close to each other, and still may
have a greater or less variation of meaning. Study some of these differences:

-ig and -lich

When attached to the same root a marked difference is noticeable between the two
adjectives. Compare:

geistig	(intellectual)	:	geistlich	(spiritual, religious)
geschäftig	(busy, active)	:	geschäftlich	(commercial)
zeitig	(early, mature)	:	zeitlich	(temporal)

Synonymous formations are scarce:

schaurig or schauerlich	-	horrible, horrid
mitternächtig or mitternächtlich	-	midnight

-ig and -en

A difference can be seen in their application to names of materials, -ig meaning
likeness, -en meaning "made of".

seidig	(silklike, silky)	:	seiden	(made of silk)
steinig	(stony, rocky)	:	steinern	(made of stone)
goldig	(dear, cute)	:	golden	(golden)

-isch and -lich

When added to the same stem they designate different aspects of a characteristic,
the former often taking on a derogatory sense. Compare:

kindisch	(childish)	:	kindlich	(childlike); in a good sense!
bäuerisch	(boorish)	:	bäuerlich	(rural, rustic)
parteiisch	(prejudiced, biased)	:	parteilich	(partial)

Practice 64 :

Fill in the blank spaces with one of the adjectival suffixes listed below. No
suffix must be used twice.

1. ein Mensch, der an nichts glaubt   ein glaubens . . .er Mensch
2. ein Tag ohne Fieber   ein fieber . . .er Tag
3. eine Steppe mit vielen Bäumen   eine baum . . .e Steppe
4. eine Zigarette mit wenig Nikotin   eine nikotin . . .e Zigarette
5. ein Gesicht mit viel Ausdruck   ein ausdrucks . . .es Gesicht
6. ein Kleid aus Wolle   ein woll . . .es Kleid
7. ein Pokal aus Glas   ein gläs . . .er Pokal
8. ein Haar wie Seide   ein seid . . .es Haar
9. das Leben auf Erden   das ird . . .e Leben
10. ein Geschäft, das Vorteile bringt   ein vorteil . . .es Geschäft
11. ein Text, den man lesen kann   ein leser . . .er Text
12. ein Mensch, der gern etwas mitteilt   ein mitteil . . .er Mensch
                 (communicate)

a. -arm   b. -en   c. -ern   d. -frei   e. -haft   f. -ig   g. -isch   h. -lich
i. -los   j. -reich   k. -sam   l. -voll

k. Adverbial Suffixes

Instead of assuming the simple uninflected form of the adjective a German adverb
sometimes takes on a specific adverbial suffix. The following suffixes are most
often used:

-falls   means as much as "in case"

     bestenfalls   -   at best
     jedenfalls   -   in any case, at any rate
     keinesfalls   -   by no means, not at all

-mal   denotes time and occassion

diesmal	- this time	zweimal	- twice, two times
manchmal	- sometimes	hundertmal	- hundred times
nochmal	- once more	vielmal(s)	- many times

-s   and   -ens

The suffix -s is affixed to nouns, adjectives and numerals. -en is only
employed with superlative forms.

abends	- in the evening	meistens	- mostly
sonntags	- on Sundays	höchstens	- at the most, at best
tagsüber	- during the day	frühestens	- at the earliest
besonders	- particularly	zweitens	- secondly, in the second
rechts	- on (to) the right		place

Adverbs ending in -s or -ens often replace longer prepositional phrases, e.g.

mangels	=	aus Mangel an	(for lack of)
eilends	=	in grosser Eile	(quickly, in haste)
flugs	=	wie im Flug	(quickly, swiftly)
mittags	=	zu Mittag	(at noon)
beiderseits	=	auf beiden Seiten	(on both sides)
unterwegs	=	auf dem Weg	(on the way)

-wärts designates direction toward

auswärts	- outwards, out of doors, abroad	vorwärts	- forward, onward
		rückwärts	- backward(s)
seitwärts	- **sideways**	ostwärts	- eastward

-weise indicates manner; sometimes the suffix is preceded by an -er or an -s

beispielsweise	- for example
paarweise	- in twos, by pairs
teilweise	- partly, in part
leihweise	- on loan
glücklicherweise	- fortunately
seltsamerweise	- strangely enough

-massen and -lei are equivalent to -weise

folgendermassen - as follows	beiderlei	- of both kinds
bekanntermassen - as is well known	allerlei	- all kinds of

Practice 65 :

Form adverbs from the words below using the suffixes indicated, and state the English meanings. Connectives are given in parentheses.

with	-falls:	ander(en)	(other)
		gleich	(equal, like)
		schlimmst(en)	(worst)
with	-s:	besonder	(special)
		link	(left)
		recht	(right)
		weiter	(further)
		Mittel	(means)
		Nachmittag	(afternoon)
		Winter	(winter)
		Zweck	(purpose)
with	-ens:	best	(best)
		mindest	(least)
		längst	(latest)
		schnellst	(fastest)

with -weise: dumm(er)   (foolish)
           unglücklich(er) (unfortunate)
           leihen   (loan); drop -en
           Gruppen   (groups)
           Massen   (masses)
           Versuch(s)   (attempt, **experiment**, **trial**)

6. Formation of Verbs by Means of Suffixes

A large number of German verbs are formed from other words, especially from nouns
and adjectives by adding the infinitive ending -en (-n) to the base word. Verbs
so derived are usually weak and regular.

a. The Infinitive Ending "-(e)n"

The following groups illustrate some of the various semantic types of
derivative verbs. In each of these categories the stem word is the basis
for a different semantic structure.

a 1. Verbs from Nouns

schneidern	(exercise the trade of a tailor)	- sich als Schneider betätigen
schlossern	(do locksmith's work)	- Schlosser
tischlern	(do cabinetmaker's work)	- Tischler
schauspielern	(play-act)	- Schauspieler
büffeln	(study hard)	- arbeiten wie ein Büffel (buffalo)
hamstern	(hoard)	- Hamster
robben	(move like a seal, crawl)	- Robbe
berlinern	(talk like a Berliner)	- Berliner
filmen	(shoot a film)	- einen Film machen
knechten	(enslave)	- Knecht (slave)
heuen	(make hay)	- Heu
mauern	(make a wall, lay bricks)	- Mauer
kleiden	(clothe, cover with clothes)	- mit Kleidern versehen
füttern	(feed animals)	- Futter
salzen	(to salt)	- Salz
zuckern	(to sugar)	- Zucker
bürsten	(to brush, use a brush)	- die Bürste benützen
bremsen	(brake, put on the brake)	- Bremse
hämmern	(to hammer)	- Hammer
schaufeln	(to shovel)	- Schaufel
häuten	(to skin, remove the skin)	- die Haut abziehen, entfernen
köpfen	(behead, decapitate)	- Kopf
schälen	(peel)	- Schale (skin, shell, husk)
schuppen	(to strip of scales)	- Schuppe (scale)

- 75 -

rosten	(to rust)	- Rost entsteht (rust is being formed)
buttern	(churn)	- Butter
dampfen	(to steam)	- Dampf
knospen	(to bud)	- Knospe (bud)

a 2. Verbs from Adjectives

kürzen	(shorten, make short)	- kurz machen
säubern	(to clean)	- sauber
töten	(kill)	- tot
zähmen	(to tame)	- zahm

faulen	(rot, become rotten)	- faul werden
grünen	(to green, become green)	- grün
reifen	(ripen, mature)	- reif
sich regen	(move)	- rege (active, busy)

bangen	(be anxious, worried)	- bange sein
lahmen	(be lame)	- lahm
kranken	**(be sick, ailing)**	- krank
wachen	(be awake)	- wach

Notice that nouns and adjectives ending in -e, -el, and -er only add
-n to the base word:

knospen	-	die Knospe
dunkeln	-	dunkel
säubern	-	sauber

Practice 66 :

Replace the expressions below with simple verbs formed from substantival bases.

das Nachtmahl essen	-	. . . .	(eat supper)
die Krone aufsetzen	-	(-"-)	(to crown)
das Gras fressen	-		(graze)
wie ein Ochs arbeiten	-		**(work very hard)**
Ketten anlegen	-		(to chain)
in der Gondel fahren	-		(row in a gondola)
die Geige spielen	-		(play the violin)
der Luft aussetzen	-	(-"-)	(to air, ventilate)
mit Farbe versehen	-	(-"-)	(to dye, color)
mit Sohlen versehen	-		(to sole)
die Feile benützen	-		(to file, smooth)
Kleckse machen	-		(to blot)

Practice 67 :

Replace the expressions below with simple verbs formed from adjectives.

ander(s) machen	-	. . . .(-"-)	(to change)
braun machen	-	(-"-)	(to brown)

glatt machen	-	(-"-)	(to smooth, polish)
krumm machen	-	(-"-)	(to bend)
locker machen	-		(loosen)
scharf machen	-	(-"-)	(sharpen)
dunkel werden	-		(get dark)
heil werden (heil machen)	-		(become sound, heal)
kühl werden (kühl machen)	-		(to cool, chill)
nass werden (nass machen)	-	(-"-)	(get wet, make wet)

b. Transitive Verbs Derived from Intransitive Verbs

Transitive weak verbs may be derived from past tense stems of intransitive
strong verbs through some change of vowel or consonant. For example "führen"
(to make go, to lead) is formed from "fuhr", the past tense of "fahren"(to go).
There is a similar situation in English:

to fall ⟶ past tense :	fell	=	transitive verb:	to fell
to lie	lay			to lay
to sit	sat		a ⟩ e	to set

Intransitive Verbs (irregular)   Transitive Verbs (regular)

liegen, lag	(lie, be situated) :	legen		(lay, put)
sinken, sank	(sink, drop) :	senken		(sink, lower)
sitzen, sass	(sit) :	setzen		(set, put)
winden, wand	(wind) :	wenden		(turn)
schwimmen, schwamm	(swim) :	schwemmen		(wash, float)
dringen, drang	(get through, penetrate into) :	drängen		(push, press)
fallen, fiel	(fall) :	fällen		(fell)
saugen, sog	(suck) :	säugen		(suckle, nurse)
fahren, fuhr	(drive, ride) :	führen		(transport, lead)
trinken, trank	(drink) :	tränken		(water, soak)
schwinden	(disappear,vanish) :	verschwenden		(waste)

c. The Suffix "-eln"

This suffix, when attached to adjectives, nouns and other verbs, forms verbs
expressing a diminutive idea, sometimes in a derogatory sense, or denoting
repetition of movements.

blöd	-	blödeln	stupid, dull	-	behave in a silly way, talk nonsense
klug	-	klügeln	clever, wise	-	subtilize
krank	-	kränkeln	sick	-	be sickly
fromm	-	frömmeln	pious	-	affect piety
das Auge	-	äugeln	eye	-	ogle
der Frost	-	frösteln	chill, frost	-	be chilly
der Tand	-	tändeln	trifles	-	trifle
der Tropfen	-	tröpfeln	drop	-	drip, trickle

husten	-	hüsteln	cough	-	cough slightly
klingen	-	klingeln	sound	-	ring
lachen	-	lächeln	laugh	-	smile
sausen	-	säuseln	hurtle, whistle	-	rustle
spotten	-	spötteln	mock, scoff	-	sneer, jeer
tanzen	-	tänzeln	dance	-	trip, frisk

Practice 68 :

Replace the expressions below with simple verbs ending in -eln.

1. den Schwanz hin und her bewegen   (-"-) . . . .   (wag)
2. sich wie eine Schlange bewegen   (-"-)   (twist, wind)
3. kleine Haufen machen   (-"-)   (pile up)
4. wiederholt bitten   (i>e)   (beg)
5. Witze machen   (wisecrack, affect wit)
6. kleine Stücke machen   (use zer-)   (cut into pieces)
7. eine Krise ist bevorstehend   (a crisis is developing)
8. in kleine Falten legen   (-"-)   (pleat)
9. sich wie eine Krabbe bewegen   (crawl)
10. durch die Nase sprechen   (-"-)   (speak through the nose)

d. The Suffix "-ern"

Verbs ending in -ern have a capability of intensifying the action expressed
in the corresponding verbs in -en :

einschlafen	-	einschläfern	fall asleep	-	put asleep
folgen	-	folgern	follow	-	conclude, infer
laufen (past:lief)	-	liefern	run	-	deliver
rauchen	-	räuchern	smoke	-	smoke, fumigate
steigen	-	steigern	climb	-	step up, increase

-ern also forms verbs expressive of sound and movement, corresponding to
English verbs in -er. However, such verbs are not suffixal derivations.
Examples are:

flackern	-	flicker	stottern	-	stutter
glitzern	-	glitter	plappern	-	babble, chatter
schimmern	-	glimmer	schnattern	-	chatter

e. The Suffix "-igen"

-igen converts adjectives and nouns into verbs:

fest	-	festigen	firm	-	secure, strengthen
rein	-	reinigen	pure, clean	-	purify, cleanse
satt	-	sättigen	satisfied	-	satisfy, satiate
die Angst	-	ängstigen	fear	-	to alarm
die Pein	-	peinigen	pain	-	torment
das Ende	-	endigen	the end	-	to end, finish

The suffix is often used with verb prefixes:

die Erde	- beerdigen	soil, earth	- bury
der Mut	- ermutigen	courage	- encourage
der Schein	- bescheinigen	certificate	- certify, attest
die Schuld	- beschuldigen	guilt, blame	- accuse, charge
	- entschuldigen		- to excuse
die Sicht	- besichtigen	sight	- to view
der Teil	- beteiligen	part, share	- give a person a share
	- sich beteiligen		- participate

f. The Suffix "-ieren"

-ieren is the only verbal suffix of foreign origin that is frequently used
in German. It is affixed especially to Latin word stems that occur in both
English and German. See page 7, # 3.

Occasionally the suffix is also attached to German stems:

das Amt	- amtieren	the office	- hold office, officiate
der Buchstabe	- buchstabieren	the letter	- spell
halb	- halbieren	half	- halve
die Spende	- spendieren	gift	- **give amply, liberally**

Practice 69 :

Give the English meaning:

abstrahieren	forcieren	nummerieren
addieren	formulieren	operieren
sich amüsieren	funktionieren	polieren
anglisieren	harmonieren	probieren
dekorieren	kommandieren	protestieren
demolieren	komponieren	rationalisieren
denunzieren	korrigieren	respektieren
deprimieren	kritisieren	simplifizieren
diskutieren	marschieren	synchronisieren
experimentieren	notieren	telegrafieren

II.   FORMATION OF WORDS THROUGH PREFIXES

In this chapter the use of the word "prefix" is restricted to particles which have
no independent existence as words. Prefixes may be divided into those used with
substantives and adjectives and those with verbs.

1. Noun And Adjective Prefixes

The German language once possessed several prefixes used with nouns and adjectives.
Today only four are still in active use: erz-, miss-, un- and ur-.

a. The Prefix "erz-"

The meaning of erz- is arch, chief, principal. The particle is prefixed to substantives denoting the holder of an office, e.g. Erzbischof (archbishop), Erzherzog (archduke). Today it is used in a wider sense to express the ultimate of a kind, often with pejorative meaning:

erzdumm	-	extremely stupid
erzfaul	-	extremely lazy
erzkonservativ	-	highly conservative
der Erzfeind	-	archenemy
ein Erzgauner	-	an arrant rogue
ein Erzlügner	-	an archliar

b. The Prefix "miss-"

Miss-, cognate with English mis as in mistake, conveys the meaning badly, wrongly, amiss, in other words, it expresses the (negative) opposite. Examples are:

der Erfolg	-	der Misserfolg	success	-	failure
die Ernte	-	die Missernte	harvest	-	bad harvest
die Gestalt	-	die Missgestalt	form, figure	-	deformity, mis-shapen figure
die Stimmung	-	die Misstimmung	humor	-	bad humor
die Tat	-	die Missetat	deed	-	misdeed
das Verhältnis	-	das Missverhältnis	proportion	-	disproportion
gefällig	-	missgefällig	pleasing	-	displeasing
(gut) gelaunt	-	missgelaunt	good-humored	-	ill-humored
gelungen	-	misslungen	successful	-	unsuccessful
(schön) gestaltet	-	missgestaltet	well-shaped	-	misshapen, deformed

The prefixes "fehl-" and "irr-" are parallel with "miss-":

Fehlgeburt	-	miscarriage	Irrlehre	-	false doctrine
Fehlentscheidung	-	wrong decision	Irrweg	-	wrong way
Fehlkalkulation	-	miscalculation	Irrglaube	-	heresy

c. The Prefix "un-"

Un-, equivalent to English un-, is the most active among the aforementioned noun and adjective prefixes. Its basic meaning is "not". It has the following functions:

c 1. Its primary function is to reverse the meaning of a word:

der Dank	-	der Undank	gratitude	-	ingratitude
die Ruhe	-	die Unruhe	rest, repose	-	unrest, un-easiness
der Sinn	-	der Unsinn	sense	-	nonsense
die Sicherheit	-	die Unsicherheit	security	-	insecurity

frei	-	unfrei	free	-	unfree
gewiss	-	ungewiss	certain	-	uncertain
wichtig	-	unwichtig	important	-	unimportant
gekünstelt	-	ungekünstelt	affected	-	unaffected

The prefix "un-" sometimes coincides with the suffix "-los". Compare these examples:

unschuldig,	schuldlos	-	innocent
untreu,	treulos	-	unfaithful
unsittlich,	sittenlos	-	immoral
untätig,	tatenlos	-	inactive
unwirksam,	wirkungslos	-	ineffective

c 2. Un- carries a negative (derogatory) connotation:

das Ding	-	das Unding	thing	-	absurdity
der Fall	-	der Unfall	the fall, event	-	accident
der Mensch	-	der Unmensch	man	-	monster, brute
die Tat	-	die Untat	deed	-	misdeed, crime
das Wetter	-	das Unwetter	weather	-	bad (stormy) weather
der Wille	-	der Unwille	the will	-	indignation, displeasure

c 3. The prefix un- is used as an intensifier:

die Menge	-	die Unmenge	amount	-	vast amount, lots of
die Summe	-	die Unsumme	sum	-	immense sum
die Tiefe	-	die Untiefe	depth	-	great depth
die Zahl	-	die Unzahl	number	-	great number

Practice 70 :

Change the meaning of the following nouns from positive to negative and give the English meanings.

Model: der Sinn (sense)   - der Unsinn (nonsense)
        die Sicherheit (security) - die Unsicherheit (insecurity)

die Aufmerksamkeit	(attention)
die Bequemlichkeit	(convenience)
der Friede	(peace)
der Gehorsam	(obedience)
die Gleichheit	(equality)
das Glück	(fortune, good luck)
die Gunst	(favor)
das Recht	(justice)
der Segen	(blessing)
die Sitte	(custom, habit)
die Treue	(loyalty)
die Tugend	(virtue)
das Vermögen	(ability, capacity)

die Vernunft	(reason)
die Wahrheit	(truth)
die Zufriedenheit	(satisfaction)

Practice 71 :

Change the following relative clauses into participial adjectives with un-.

Model: ein Haus, das nicht bewohnt ist   - ein unbewohntes Haus
        ein Gast, der nicht erwünscht ist - ein unerwünschter Gast

   1. ein Dichter, der nicht bekannt ist
   2. ein Mädchen, das nicht verheiratet ist
   3. Menschen, die keine Bildung haben
   4. ein Leben, das ohne Ordnung ist
   5. Jugend, die nicht verstanden wird
   6. Hände, die nicht gewaschen sind
   7. Bücher, die nicht gelesen werden
   8. Briefmarken, die nicht gestempelt sind
   9. Edelsteine, die nicht geschliffen sind
  10. Grenzen, die nicht geschützt sind

Practice 72 :

In accordance with the model complete the following sentences by supplying
adjectives prefixed with un- and ending in -bar, resp. -lich .

A) Model : Was man nicht brauchen kann, ist unbrauchbar. (useless)

1. Was man nicht zerstören kann, ist		(indestructible)
2. Was man nicht zählen kann, ist		(innumerable)
3. Was man nicht sagen kann, ist		(unspeakable)
4. Was man nicht berechnen kann, ist	**(-enbar)**	(incalculable)
5. Was man nicht schätzen kann, ist		(inestimable)
6. Was man nicht trennen kann, ist		(inseparable)
7. Was man nicht denken kann, ist		(unthinkable)
8. Was man nicht tragen kann, ist		(unbearable)
9. Was man nicht lösen kann, ist		(unsolvable)
10. Was man nicht heilen kann, ist		(incurable)

B) Model: Was man nicht ersetzen kann, ist unersetzlich.(irreplaceable)

1. Was man nicht bewegen kann, ist		(immovable)
2. Was man nicht abändern kann, ist		(unalterable)
3. Was man nicht zerbrechen kann, ist		(unbreakable)
4. Was man nicht aussprechen kann, ist		(inexpressible)
5. Was man nicht glauben kann, ist		(incredible)
6. Was man nicht beschreiben kann, ist		(indescribable)
7. Was man nicht lesen kann, ist	**(-erlich)**	(illegible)
8. Was man nicht begreifen kann, ist		(incomprehensible)
9. Was man nicht ausstehen kann, ist		(intolerable)
10. Was man nicht entbehren kann, ist		(indispensable)

d. The Prefix "ur-"

Ur- means <u>original</u>, <u>primitive</u>, <u>very old</u>. Examples are :

der Uranfang	-	first beginning
die Uraufführung	-	first night (performance)
die Urbewohner	-	aborigines
der Urgrossvater	-	great-grandfather
die Urzeit	-	primitive times

Ur- has often the force of <u>very</u>, <u>extremely</u> :

uralt	-	very old, very ancient
urkomisch	-	extremely funny
urplötzlich	-	all of a sudden
ursprünglich	-	original, primitive

2. Verb Prefixes

Derivative verbs are formed with the following prefixes : <u>be-</u>, <u>ent-</u>, <u>er-</u>, <u>ge-</u>, <u>ver-</u>, <u>zer-</u> and <u>miss-</u>. They are generally referred to as inseparable prefixes. Verbs with these prefixes are stressed on the stem syllable, not on the prefix, and the past participles do not take the prefix <u>ge-</u>. The so-called separable prefixes are adverbial in nature, and have been treated as part of word-compounding.

a. The Prefix "be-"

<u>Be-</u> (related to <u>bei</u>) expresses the idea of providing with something, giving something:

das Dach	-	bedachen	the roof	- to roof (provide with a roof)
die Decke	-	bedecken	the cover	- to cover (put a cover on)
das Kleid	-	bekleiden	the dress	- to dress (put a dress on)
das Licht	-	belichten	the light	- expose (provide with light)
der Flügel	-	beflügeln	the wing	- lend wings to
der Kranz	-	bekränzen	wreath	- wreathe (form a wreath around)
die Sohle	-	besohlen	sole	- to sole (put on soles)

The most important use of the prefix is to convert intransitive verbs into transitive verbs :

<u>Intransitive Verbs</u> (requiring a prepositional object)		<u>Transitive Verbs</u> (requiring an accusative object)	
antworten auf	(give an answer to)	beantworten	(to answer)
denken an	(think of)	bedenken	(consider)
schreiben über	(write on)	beschreiben	(describe)

sprechen über	(talk about)	besprechen	(discuss)
treten in	(step, walk into)	betreten	(enter)
weinen über	(weep over)	beweinen	(deplore)
wohnen in	(live in)	bewohnen	(occupy, inhabit)

Some transitive verbs also take the prefix <u>be</u>- to indicate completion or perfection of the idea expressed in the verb:

decken	-	bedecken	to cover	-	to cover
enden	-	beenden	to end, finish	-	to end, finish
fragen	-	befragen	ask	-	to question, interrogate
hüten	-	behüten	guard	-	protect
sehen	-	besehen	see	-	inspect, examine

Finally the prefix serves to make a verb of an adjective. See page **78**, e.

frei	-	befreien	free	-	liberate
lustig	-	belustigen	merry	-	amuse, entertain
reich	-	bereichern	rich	-	enrich
richtig	-	berichtigen	right	-	rectify
ruhig	-	beruhigen	calm, quiet	-	to calm, soothe
schuldig	-	beschuldigen	guilty	-	accuse, charge with
stark	-	bestärken	strong	-	strengthen

Practice 73 :

In the following sentences change the intransitive verbs into transitive verbs and make the necessary adjustments.

Model: Er <u>antwortet auf</u> meine Frage.   -   Er <u>beantwortet</u> meine Frage.
       Die Gäste <u>treten in</u> den Saal.   -   Die Gäste <u>betreten</u> den Saal.

1. Die Fremden staunten über die Schönheit des Landes.
2. Sie klagten über den Verlust.
3. Kannst du mir raten ?
4. Wie urteilen Sie über die politische Lage ?
5. Die Firma liefert nur an ausländische Kunden.
6. Ein mächtiger König herrschte über das Land.
7. Es ist eine sportliche Leistung, auf diesen Berg zu steigen.
8. Wer zahlt für die Getränke ?
9. Das Heer kämpfte gegen einen mächtigen Feind.
10. Können Sie für die Theaterkarten sorgen ?

Practice 74 :

From each of the nouns in parentheses form verbs with <u>be</u>- and complete the sentences.

1. Wann können Sie die Arbeit . . . . (Ende) ?
2. Es ist nicht zu . . . . . ., dass Sie recht haben (Streit).
3. Warum . . . . . . Sie meine Erklärungen (Zweifel) ?
4. Der Tote wurde gestern . . . . . . (Grab).
5. Die Soldaten . . . . . . die feindlichen Stellungen (Sturm). **(-"-)**

6. Sie haben den Film zu lange . . . .(Licht).
7. Jedes Blatt muss deutlich . . . . . . werden. (Schrift).
8. Sie sollen sich Ihr Auto neu . . . . lassen (Reifen).
9. Darf ich Sie zu Ihrer Beförderung . . . .(Glückwunsch). (-"-)
10.Wir haben uns kürzlich mit dieser Familie . . . .(Freund).

b. The Prefix "ent-"

b 1. Ent- essentially expresses the idea of separation, removal or
escape (English de-, dis-, un- and away):

falten	-	entfalten	to fold	-	unfold
fliehen	-	entfliehen	flee	-	escape
führen	-	entführen	to lead	-	carry off, abduct
lassen	-	entlassen	leave	-	dismiss, discharge
laufen	-	entlaufen	to run	-	run away
nehmen	-	entnehmen	take	-	take from, withdraw
reissen	-	entreissen	to tear	-	snatch away
fern	-	entfernen	far, distant	-	remove, withdraw
fremd	-	entfremden	strange	-	estrange

b 2. The prefix ent- denotes the beginning of an activity:

brennen	-	entbrennen	to burn	-	catch fire, become inflamed
schlafen	-	entschlafen	to sleep	-	fall asleep
springen	-	entspringen	to spring	-	arise
spriessen	-	entspriessen	to sprout	-	sprout, spring up
stehen	-	entstehen	to stand	-	arise, originate

Practice 75 :

Form verbs denoting separation by adding ent- to the following nouns.

Model: dem Menschen den Mut wegnehmen   - den Menschen entmutigen (discourage)
       dem Denkmal die Hülle wegnehmen - das Denkmal enthüllen (unveil)

1. dem Körper die Kraft wegnehmen	(ä)	(weaken, devitalize)
2. dem Verbrecher die Waffe w.		(disarm)
3. dem Meerwasser das Salz w.		(desalt)
4. dem Baum die Blätter w.		(defoliate)
5. der Briefmarke den Wert w.		(cancel, depreciate)
6. dem Mörder das Haupt w.		(decapitate)
7. der Flasche den Kork w.		(uncork)
8. der Kirsche den Kern w.		(stone, pit)
9. dem Tier die Last w.		(unburden)
10.der Wiese das Wasser w.	(ä)	(drain)
11.dem Baum die Wurzel w.		(unroot, uproot)
12.dem Metall die Härte w.		(soften)

c. The Prefix "er-"

Er- has two main senses:

c 1. Successful completion of the action indicated by the verb; sometimes the conclusion of the action means death.

arbeiten	-	erarbeiten	to work	-	obtain by hard work
kämpfen	-	erkämpfen	to fight	-	obtain by fighting
kennen	-	erkennen	know	-	recognize
schaffen	-	erschaffen	do, work	-	create
werben	-	erwerben	sue for, solicit	-	acquire
frieren	-	erfrieren	be cold	-	freeze to death
liegen	-	erliegen	lie	-	succumb
schiessen	-	erschiessen	shoot	-	shoot dead
schlagen	-	erschlagen	to hit	-	to kill
trinken	-	ertrinken	to drink	-	drown, be drowned

With a few verbs er- denotes the beginning of the action:

blühen	-	erblühen (aufblühen)	to bloom	-	begin to bloom, flourish
klingen	-	erklingen	to ring, sound	-	resound
wachen	-	erwachen (aufwachen)	be awake	-	awake

c 2. From adjectives it forms verbs with inchoative or factitive meaning:

blass werden	or:	erblassen	grow (turn) pale
blind werden		erblinden	grow blind
kalt werden		erkalten	get cold
matt werden		ermatten	grow tired, weary
starr werden		erstarren	grow stiff, stiffen

ganz machen	or:	ergänzen	complete, replenish
heiter machen		erheitern	cheer up
hoch machen		erhöhen	raise
neu machen		erneuen (erneuern)	renew, revive
warm machen		erwärmen	warm up

Practice 76 :

Replace the verbal phrases in the sentences by verbs with er- :

Model: Sein Gesicht wurde blass.   - Sein Gesicht erblasste. (turn pale)
      Das Wetter hat mich matt gemacht. - Das Wetter hat mich ermattet. (tire)

1. Das Bad hat mich wieder frisch gemacht.   (refresh)
2. Er hat es mir möglich gemacht.   (make possible)

3. Der lange Marsch hat ihn müde gemacht. (exhaust)
4. Du machst mir die Arbeit schwer. (make more difficult)
5. Moderne Erfindungen machen uns das Leben leichter. (make easier)
6. Gib acht, dass du nicht krank wirst. (get sick)
7. Sie wurde rot bis über die Ohren. (-"-) (blush)
8. Sein Haar begann grau zu werden. (gray)
9. Meine Finger sind ganz starr geworden. (grow stiff)
10. Die Kinder werden schnell müde. (get tired)

Practice 77 :

Replace the verbs and verbal phrases in the sentences by verbs with er-
and make changes that are necessary. (Derived verbs express intensified action).

Model: Er hat um sein Recht gekämpft. - Er hat sein Recht erkämpft.
       Ich wache immer früh auf. - Ich erwache immer früh.

1. Wir bitten Sie um Ihre Hilfe.
2. Ich habe mir das Geld für ein Auto gespart.
3. Die Soldaten stürmten die Burg.
4. Er schlug ihn tot.
5. Wir mussten den Hund totschiessen.
6. Er griff nach ihrer Hand.
7. Wir hoffen alle auf bessere Zeiten.
8. Sie haben sich nach dem Wiedersehen mit uns gesehnt.
9. Er arbeitete für ein eigenes Häuschen.
10. Du hast den besten Teil gewählt.
11. Ich warte auf dich um 10 Uhr in der Bibliothek.
12. Der Arzt forschte nach den Ursachen der Krankheit.

d. The Prefix "ge-"

Only a small number of verbs with ge- have survived, and the meaning of
the prefix is no longer discernible. Today ge- has mainly come to be the
sign of the past participle.

e. The Prefix "ver-"

The prefix ver- has a variety of functions :

e 1. It serves as a means of converting nouns and adjectives (including
comparatives) into verbs, often with inchoative and factitive meaning.

alt werden or:	veraltern	become obsolete, go out of date
arm werden	verarmen	become poor
blass werden	verblassen	fade
einsam werden	vereinsamen	become lonely
trocken werden	vertrocknen	dry up
welk werden	verwelken	fade, wither
zu Dampf werden	verdampfen	evaporate
zu Kalk werden	verkalken	calcify, harden
zu Stein werden	versteinern	turn into stone, petrify
zu Rost werden	verrosten	to rust

billig machen	or:	verbilligen	lower the prices, cheapen
dunkel machen		verdunkeln	make dark, darken
dünn machen		verdünnen	to thin, dilute
kleiner machen		verkleinern	make smaller, reduce
länger machen		verlängern	lengthen, prolong
mehr machen		vermehren	increase, augment
zu Kohle machen		verkohlen	carbonize, char
zu Koks machen		verkoken	to coke
zu einem Film machen		verfilmen	to film

e 2. From nouns it forms verbs with the meaning of <u>provide with</u>:

mit Gold überziehen	or:	vergolden	to plate with gold, gild
mit Silber überziehen		versilbern	to silver coat
mit Eis überziehen		vereisen	to ice up
mit Chrom überziehen		verchromen	to chromium plate
mit Glas überziehen		verglasen	to glaze
mit Minen versehen		verminen	to mine
mit einem Siegel verschliessen		versiegeln	to seal
mit Staub bedeckt werden		verstauben	get dusty

<u>Practice 78</u> :

Replace the predicate in the phrases by verbs with <u>ver-</u> .

Model: eine Flüssigkeit dünn machen   - eine Flüssigkeit verdünnen (thin down)
       das Leben länger machen   - das Leben verlängern (prolong)

etwas deutlich machen
seine Kenntnisse vollkommen machen
eine Sache einfach machen
die Suppe dick machen
die Industrie staatlich machen
die Speise süss machen
die Milch wässerig machen   (stem : <u>wässer-</u>)
das Bild grösser machen
die Strasse breiter machen
die Luft besser machen
die Landschaft schöner machen
den Abstand kürzer machen   (stem : <u>kürz-</u>)
den Graben tiefer machen   (stem : <u>tief-</u>)
einen Ton stärker machen   (stem : <u>stärk-</u>)

e 3. <u>Ver-</u> changes the meaning of verbs in many ways :

A. <u>Reversal of meaning ; doing the thing the wrong way</u>

achten	-	verachten	esteem, respect	- despise
fahren	-	sich verfahren	drive	- go the wrong way
führen	-	verführen	guide, lead	- seduce
kaufen	-	verkaufen	buy	- sell
legen	-	verlegen	place, put	- misplace
lernen	-	verlernen	learn	- forget
mieten	-	vermieten	rent, hire	- hire (out),lease,let
rechnen	-	sich verrechnen	calculate	- miscalculate, be mistaken
sprechen	-	sich versprechen	speak	- make a slip of the tongue

B. <u>Idea of completion or progress to destruction</u>

brauchen	-	verbrauchen	to use	- use up, consume
brennen	-	verbrennen	burn	- burn up; spoil by burning
heilen	-	verheilen	heal	- heal **completely**
hungern	-	verhungern	to hunger	- starve to death
rauchen	-	verrauchen	to smoke	- go off in smoke
sinken	-	versinken	to sink	- sink down, sink completely
spielen	-	verspielen	to play,gamble	- gamble away, lose
wischen	-	verwischen	wipe	- wipe out, efface
zweifeln	-	verzweifeln	to doubt	- despair

C. <u>Idea of "away, forth"</u>; verbs often express various ways time is spent

bringen	-	verbringen	bring	- spend (one's time)
geben	-	vergeben	give	- give away, give out
gehen	-	vergehen	go	- pass away, fade
reisen	-	verreisen	travel	- go on a journey, go away, leave
schenken	-	verschenken	give, make a present-	give away
senden	-	versenden	send	- dispatch, forward
träumen	-	verträumen	to dream	- dream away
treiben	-	vertreiben	to drive, press	- drive away
trinken	-	vertrinken	to drink	- spend in drinking

<u>Practice 79</u> :

Determine the English meaning of the following verbs with <u>ver-</u>, all of which imply
an undesirable effect or the idea of error:

Die Suppe ist versalzen.
Da habe ich mich wohl verhört.
Wo hast du mein Buch versteckt ?
Sie hat mir den Kopf verdreht.
Wir haben den Ernst der Lage verkannt.

- 89 -

Du hast dich wieder im Brief verschrieben.
Ich habe mir den Fuss vertreten.
Das Klavier ist ganz verstimmt.
Man soll die Kinder nicht verwöhnen.
Die Kinder haben sich im Wald verlaufen.
Das Bild hängt verkehrt **an** der Wand.
Du musst dich verlesen haben.
Er verschläft sich fast jeden Morgen.
Er hat sein ganzes Geld vertan.
Die beiden Jungen sind leicht zu verwechseln.

Practice 80 :

Put the prefix <u>ver-</u> before the verbs in the following sentences, hereby implying that the action is coming to a destructive completion. Give the English meaning of the verbs:

Model : Die Blume <u>blüht</u> . (bloom)   -   Die Blume <u>verblüht</u>. **(wilt)**

Die Blätter welken schon. **(wilt)**
Das Holz fault. (rot)
Die Musik klingt. (sound)
Das Tier durstet. (be thirsty)
Das Feuer glüht im Ofen. (glow)
Das Brot schimmelt. (get moldy)
Die alten Häuser fallen. (fall)
Das Kind blutet. (bleed)
Das Echo hallt. (sound)

f. The Prefix "zer-"

The prefix <u>zer-</u> denotes destructive action, often one of separating or going to pieces. It forms verbs chiefly from other verbs and from a few nouns:

der Brocken	-	zerbröckeln	fragment, crumb	-	crumble
der Staub	-	zerstäuben	dust	-	pulverize, spray
das Stück	-	zerstückeln	piece, bit	-	to cut into pieces
die Trümmer	-	zertrümmern	ruins, rubble	-	lay in ruins, demolish
brechen	-	zerbrechen	to break	-	break up, break to pieces
fallen	-	zerfallen	to fall	-	fall to pieces, decay
setzen	-	zersetzen	to set	-	decompose
springen	-	zerspringen	to crack	-	to burst
teilen	-	zerteilen	divide	-	divide up, disperse
trennen	-	zertrennen	separate	-	rip up

Practice 81 :

Give the English meaning of the following "zer-" verbs:

1. die Uhr zerlegen
2. das Holz zerkleinern
3. den Satz zergliedern

4. den Kuchen zerschneiden
5. den Brief zerreissen
6. das Fenster zerschlagen
7. die Rose zerpflücken
8. den Tisch zersägen
9. das Gemüse zerkochen
10. die Herde zersprengen
11. das Gras zertrampeln
12. den Wurm zertreten

g. The Prefix "miss-"

Miss-, meaning wrong, false, has some of the qualities of an inseparable prefix.
See also page **80**, par. b.

Note that the prefixes be-, ge- and ver- are sometimes omitted before miss-.

beachten	-	missachten	notice, pay attention	- disregard, neglect
deuten	-	missdeuten	interpret	- misinterpret
behagen	-	missbehagen	please	- displease
gelingen	-	misslingen		
glücken	-	missglücken	succeed	- fail, not succeed
geraten	-	missraten	turn out (all right)	- turn out wrong

Practice 82 :

Change the meaning of the following words by putting the prefix miss- before, and
give the English equivalents:

(be)handeln   (treat)
die (Be)handlung   (treatment)

bilden   (to form)
die Bildung   (formation, shape)

billigen   (approve)
die Billigung   (approval)

(ge)brauchen   (to use)
der (Ge)brauch   (the use, usage)

(ge)fallen   (please, like)
der (Ge)fallen   (pleasure, favor)

gönnen   (to grant)
die Gunst   (favor)

(ver)trauen   (to trust)
das (Ver)trauen   (trust, confidence)

verstehen   (understand)
das Verständnis   (understanding)

vergnügt   (pleased, delighted)
das Vergnügen   (pleasure)

3. Summary of Verbal Prefixes

The following tables are intended to give a final comprehensive view of all the verbal prefixes that have been discussed at full length. See also page 30, # 5 a.

a. Synonymous Prefixes (Partial synonymity !)

Prefix	Synonym for				
be-	aus-	berechnen	-	ausrechnen	(calculate)
		befragen	-	ausfragen	(interrogate)
	er-	besteigen	-	ersteigen	(ascend, scale)
		bewirken	-	erwirken	(effect)
	über-	begiessen	-	übergiessen	(pour over)
		bedecken	-	überdecken	(overlay)
	um-	begehen	-	umgehen	(walk around)
		belagern	-	umlagern	(besiege)
ent-	ab-	entrahmen	-	abrahmen	(skim milk)
		entstammen	-	abstammen	(descend from)
	aus-	s.entkleiden	-	s.auskleiden	(undress)
		entleeren	-	ausleeren	(empty)
	weg-	entlaufen	-	weglaufen	(run away)
		entreissen	-	wegreissen	(tear away)
er-	auf-	erblühen	-	aufblühen	(begin to bloom)
		erwachen	-	aufwachen	(wake up)
	aus-	erdenken	-	ausdenken	(think out, devise)
		erwählen	-	auswählen	(choose)
ver-	ab-	verschliessen	-	abschliessen	(close)
		verblassen	-	abblassen	(fade)
	auf-	verschieben	-	aufschieben	(delay)
		verbrauchen	-	aufbrauchen	(use up)
	aus-	verbleichen	-	ausbleichen	(fade)
		verteilen	-	austeilen	(distribute)
	be-	verdecken	-	bedecken	(cover)
		verstärken	-	bestärken	(strengthen)
	miss-, fehl-	verleiten	-	missleiten	(mislead)
		verdrucken	-	fehldrucken	(misprint)

zer-	verfallen	-	zerfallen	(decay)
	verstreuen	-	zerstreuen	(scatter, disperse)
zu-	vernageln	-	zunageln	(nail up)
	verschliessen	-	zuschliessen	(lock up) *)

b. Antonymous Prefixes

See also page 31, # 5 b.

Prefix	Antonym of					
be-	ent-	bewaffnen	(arm)	:	entwaffnen	(disarm)
		beladen	(load)	:	entladen	(unload)
	miss-	beachten	(notice)	:	missachten	(disregard)
		behandeln	(treat)	:	misshandeln	(ill-treat)
er-	ent-	ermutigen	(encourage)	:	entmutigen	(discourage)
		erwischen	(get hold of)	:	entwischen	(escape)
ver-	auf-	verdecken	(cover)	:	aufdecken	(uncover)
		verblühen	(wither)	:	aufblühen	(begin to bloom)
	ent-	vergasen	(gas)	:	entgasen	(degas)
		verhüllen	(veil)	:	enthüllen	(unveil)
	er-	verklingen	(die away)	:	erklingen	(sound)
		verlernen	(forget)	:	erlernen	(learn)
	miss-	vergönnen	(not grudge)	:	missgönnen	(grudge)
		vertrauen	(trust)	:	misstrauen	(distrust)

c. Principal Sense Groups of Verbal Prefixes

In the table below the verbal prefixes are divided into groups, according to the kind of influence they exert on the meaning of the verbs. This summary should provide a final key to the understanding of the nature of these important word-building blocks.

c 1. starting an action	an-	anlaufen	-	start
		anwerfen	-	begin to throw
	los-	losschiessen	-	fire off
		losziehen	-	set out
	ent-	entbrennen	-	take fire
		entschlafen	-	fall asleep
	er-	erblühen	-	begin to bloom
		erwachen	-	awake

---

*) It is understood that interchangeability applies only to certain pairs, i.e. it is never more than partial.

(sudden beginning)	auf-	aufflammen	-	flame up
		aufleuchten	-	flash up
(progressive beginning)	ein-	einarbeiten	-	work in, train
		einfahren	-	**break in a car**

c 2. <u>finishing an action</u>

	ab-	abgeben	-	deliver
		abtragen	-	wear out
	auf-	aufessen	-	eat up
		aufräumen	-	tidy up, clear away
	aus-	ausklingen	-	cease to sound
		austrinken	-	drink up, empty
	durch-	durchkommen	-	get (come) through
		durchsägen	-	saw through
	ver-	verbrauchen	-	use up, consume
		verheilen	-	heal up

c 3. <u>duration</u>

	durch-	durchschlafen	-	sleep through
		durchtanzen	-	dance through
	zu-	zubringen	-	spend (time)
		zuhören	-	listen to
	ver-	verbringen	-	spend, pass (time)
		vertreiben	-	pass away (time)

c 4. <u>notion of approaching</u>

	an-	ankommen	-	arrive
		anschauen	-	look at
	zu-	zukommen auf	-	come up to
		zusehen	-	watch, look on

c 5. <u>intensified action</u>
(doing something thoroughly, successful completion)

	ein-	einseifen	-	soap, lather
		einüben	-	practice, train
	nach-	nachsehen	-	inspect, check
		nachsinnen	-	ponder, muse
	über-	überprüfen	-	inspect, check, scrutinize
		überwachen	-	control, watch over
	um-	umwälzen	-	roll around, revolutionize
		umwandeln	-	change, transform
	be-	befragen	-	interrogate
		begrüssen	-	greet

	er-	erkämpfen	-	obtain by fighting
		erstürmen	-	take by storm
	ver-	verbrennen	-	burn up
		verhungern	-	starve to death
	zer-	zerfliessen	-	dissolve, melt
		zerteilen	-	divide up
(overdoing the action)	über-	übertreiben	-	overdo, exaggerate
		übervölkern	-	overpopulate

c 6. <u>idea of "get, become , grow"</u>

	ab-	abkühlen	-	cool off
		abmagern	-	grow lean, thin
	er-	ergrauen	-	become grey, gray
		erkalten	-	get cold, cool down
	ver-	veralten	-	become obsolete
		vereinsamen	-	become lonely

c 7. <u>idea of "make, turn into"</u>

	be-	befreien	-	free, liberate
		berichtigen	-	rectify, correct
	er-	ermöglichen	-	make possible
		erneuern	-	renew, revive
	ver-	verdunkeln	-	make dark, darken
		verkleinern	-	make smaller, reduce

c 8. <u>idea of "providing with"</u>

	aus-	ausmöblieren	-	furnish (an apartment)
		auspolstern	-	pad, stuff
	über-	überdachen	-	put a roof on
		überkleiden	-	cover a thing over
	um-	umgittern	-	provide with a grill, fence
		ummauern	-	wall in
	be-	bekränzen	-	wreathe
		besohlen	-	sole, put on soles
	ver-	verchromen	-	chromium plate
		versilbern	-	silver coat

c 9. <u>negation, opposition</u>

	ab-	abberufen	-	recall
		abbestellen	-	cancel (orders for)

miss-	missbilligen	-	disapprove
	misslingen	-	fail, not succeed
ver-	verachten	-	despise
	verkennen	-	fail to realize
dis-	disharmonieren	-	disharmonize, not agree
	disqualifizieren	-	disqualify

c 10. <u>separation, loss,</u>
      <u>deprivation</u>

ab-	abgehen	-	go off, depart
	abliefern	-	deliver
aus-	ausquartieren	-	dislodge
	austreiben	-	drive out
fort-	fortlaufen	-	run away
weg-	wegnehmen	-	take away
um-	umbringen	-	kill
	umkommen	-	perish, die
ent-	entkleiden	-	undress
	entreissen	-	snatch away
ver-	sich verlaufen	-	lose one's way, scatter
	versenden	-	send, dispatch
zer-	zerfallen	-	fall to pieces, decay
	zerbrechen	-	break up, break to pieces

c 11. <u>idea of error</u>
      (doing something the
      wrong way)

miss-	missbrauchen	-	abuse
	misshandeln	-	ill-treat
ver-	verführen	-	seduce
	sich versprechen	-	make a slip of the tongue

c 12. <u>repetition</u>
      (doing things a
      different way)

auf-	auffärben	-	redye
	aufforsten	-	reforest
um-	umbauen	-	remodel
	umschulen	-	retrain
re-	rekonstruieren	-	reconstruct
	regenerieren	-	regenerate

Practice 83 :

From the list provided supply the missing verb which fits the given context
and change the verb form accordingly.

A. a. sich ankleiden - b. sich verkleiden - c. sich umkleiden - d. sich kleiden -
    e. sich entkleiden-

    1. Die Mädchen . . . . . . sich nach der neuesten Mode.
    2. Ich stand auf und begann mich . . . .
    3. Die Kinder . . . . . sich gern.
    4. Du musst dich für das Abendessen . . . . . .
    5. Ich . . . . mich und legte mich schlafen.

B. a. verführen - b. entführen - c. abführen - d. vorführen - e. einführen

    1. Der Dieb wurde ins Gefängnis . . . .
    2. Später wurde er dem Richter . . . .
    3. Das Kind wurde aus dem Haus . . . .
    4. Diese Waren werden aus dem Ausland . . . .
    5. Ich lasse mich nicht zum Rauchen . . . . .

C. a. befallen - b. einfallen - c. verfallen - d. vorfallen - e. entfallen

    1. Das Buch ist seinen Händen . . . . . .
    2. Die Familie wurde von einem schweren Unglück . . . . . .
    3. Dieser nette Vers ist mir heute . . . .
    4. Es ist gar nichts Neues . . . .
    5. Die meisten Häuser sind alt und . . . . . .

D. a. abhandeln - b. behandeln - c. einhandeln - d. misshandeln - e. verhandeln

    1. Er versuchte, etwas vom Preis . . . .
    2. Die Uhr habe ich mir billig . . . .
    3. Unser Hausarzt . . . . . . den Patienten.
    4. Das Komitee hat bis in die Nacht . . . . .
    5. Das Kind wurde von den Eltern schwer . . . . .

E. a. ausarbeiten - b. durcharbeiten - c. erarbeiten - d. umarbeiten -
    e. verarbeiten

    1. Hier wird Holz zu Papier . . . .
    2. Ich lasse mir meinen Ring . . . . . .
    3. Er hat sich seinen Reichtum . . . . .
    4. Sie werden noch die genauen Pläne . . . . . .
    5. Die Sekretärin musste bis acht Uhr abends . . . . .

F. a. absteigen - b. aussteigen - c. ersteigen - d. übersteigen - e. sich
    versteigen

    1. Wegen schlechter Sicht . . . . . . sich viele Wanderer in den Bergen.
    2. Ich habe die höchste Stufe des Erfolgs . . . . . .
    3. In welchem Hotel sind Sie . . . . ?
    4. Ich hoffe, unser Verlust . . . . nicht 300 Mark.
    5. Ich will zum Goetheplatz fahren. Wo muss ich . . . . . ?

4. Prefixes of Foreign Origin

The prefixes listed here have originated in Greek, Latin **or** French. They occur frequently in scientific and technical terms which have become part of practically every language in the world. Note occasional differences in the English and German spelling. See also page 5, # IV.

Prefix	Meaning	Examples
a-, an-	without, not, opposite to	asozial, anorganisch
anti-	opposite, against	Antifaschismus, antikommunistisc'
auto-	self, same, self-propelled	Autobiographie, automatisch
de-	reversal or undoing; removal	degradieren, Demaskierung
dis-	negation, lack, invalidation, deprivation (synonym of miss-)	Disharmonie, disqualifizieren
ex-	former	Exkaiser, Exweltmeister
extra-	more than usual, special	extravagant, Extraausgabe
hyper-	over, above, in great amount (Greek counterpart to Latin super-)	hyperkorrekt, Hypertonie (high blood pressure)
hypo-	below, beneath, inferior (Greek counterpart to Latin sub-)	Hypotonie (low blood pressure), Hypothermie
il-, in-, ir-	contradiction, negation	illegal, illegitim indirekt, intolerant irregulär, irrational
inter-	between, among	Intersex, international
ko-, kon-	jointly, together, mutually	Kopilot, Koexistenz Kontext, kongenial
makro-	largeness in extent, duration	Makroklima, Makrokosmos
mikro-	smaller, reduced in size	Mikrofilm, Mikrokosmos
mini-	distinctively smaller, shorter	Minikleid, Minigolf
mono-	one, single, alone	Monokultur, Monogamie
neo-	recent, new development or new formation	Neofaschismus, neogotisch
non-	simple negation	Nonstopflug, Nonkonformist
poly-	more than one, many or much	Polygamie, polychrom
prä-	earlier or prior time; before in position and importance	prähistorisch, Präposition

pseudo-	inauthenticity; sham	Pseudonym, pseudowissenschaft-lich
re-	repetition of previous action	Reproduktion, **rekonstruieren**
sub-	under, beneath, inferior	Subordination, submarin (unter-seeisch)
super-	superiority	Superbombe, superfein
vize-	substitution for; acting in place of	Vizeadmiral, Vizepräsident

5. Word Families

This text will be concluded with the presentation of what is called in German "Wortfamilien". The first table gives an illustration of the entire combinatory range of a weak verb. Here, the nucleus of all these word combinations is the stem of the verb "leben". The second example demonstrates the prolific nature of strong verbs to form derivatives by utilizing the stem of their principal parts.

Word Family of "leben" (to live)

	VERBS leben – to live	NOUNS das Leben – life	ADJECTIVES (PARTICIPLES) lebend – living, alive
PREFIX	ableben – die aufleben – live again, be cheered up sich ausleben – live one's full life beleben – revive, animate sich einleben – accustom oneself erleben – experience fortleben – live on miterleben – join an experience nachleben – live later, survive überleben – outlive, survive vorleben – demonstrate verleben – spend, pass	das Ableben – death das Erleben – experience das Fortleben (nach) – life after das Nachleben – afterlife der Überlebende – survivor das Vorleben – former life, past	abgelebt – worn out, decrepit belebt – lively, animated überlebt – antiquated verlebt – worn out
SUFFIX		die Lebendigkeit – liveliness, vividness die Lebhaftigkeit – vividness die Leblosigkeit – lifelessness	lebendig – living, alive lebhaft – lively, vivid leblos – lifeless -lebig – -lived
PREFIX plus SUFFIX	verlebendigen – make lively, spirited	die Abgelebtheit – **decrepitude** die Belebung – enlivenment die Belebtheit – animation, liveliness das Erlebnis – experience, occurrence	
COMPOUNDS	hochleben (lassen) – salute, give a person a cheer	das Belebungs-mittel – restorative die Lebensdauer – life span	kurzlebig – short-lived

die Lebensgefahr – danger of life	lebensgefähr-lich – perilous	
die Lebenslust – love of life	lebenslustig – enjoying life, jolly	
die Leichtlebig-keit – lighthearted-ness	leichtlebig – easy-going	
die Lebensfähig-keit – fitness for life	lebensfähig – fit to live	

Word Family of "binden" (to tie, bind)

	binden	band	gebunden
VERBS	abbinden – untie, unbind	bündern – form into ribbons	bündeln – bundle
	anbinden – tie to	bündigen – tame	verbünden – bind, join, connect
	aufbinden – tie up		
	einbinden – bind (book)		
	losbinden – untie		
	umbinden – tie around, put on		
	unterbinden – stop		
	zubinden – tie up		
	zusammenbinden – tie together		
	entbinden – dispense, re-lease		
	verbinden – connect, unite		
	festbinden – fasten		
NOUNS	die Binde – band, sling, tie	das Band – ribbon, tape	das Bund – bundle, bunch
	der Binder – binder, tie	der Band – volume	der Bund – band; union, league, **federal**
	die Bindung – binding	die Bande – gang, band	

NOUNS		
die Entbindung- – dispensation	die Bündigung – taming	das Bündel – bundle
das Gebinde – bundle	der Einband – bookcover	die Bündigkeit – conciseness
die Unterbin- dung – disconnection	der Verband – bandage; association	das Bündnis – alliance
die Verbindung- – connection	der Bandwurm – tapeworm	der Ausbund – model, paragon
die Verbindlich- keit – obligation	das Tonband – recording tape	das Bundesland – Federal State
das Bindewort – conjunction	das Stimmband – vocal cord	die Bundes- republik – Federal Republic
der Buchbinder – book**binder**	der Löwen- bändiger – lion tamer	der Schlüssel- bund – bunch of keys
die Studenten- verbindung- – fraternity	der Verband- kasten – first-aid kit	die Verbunden- heit – solidarity, unity
das Entbindungs- heim – maternity home		die Verbündeten- – allies
	der Völkerbundverband – League of Nations Union	

ADJECT. PARTI- CIPLES		
bündend ⎫ verbindlich ⎭ – binding, obligatory	-bündig – in .... volumes	bündig – binding; concise
	vierbündig – in four volumes	verbündet – allied
	unbündig – insubordinate	bundbrüchig – disloyal to an agreement
		kurz angebunden- short, abrupt

Practice 84 :

In the blank spaces of each line insert the derivatives that can be formed from the stem of the words underlined and the given affixes. Umlaut and need for vowel change are indicated. Also give the English meanings.

VERBS	NOUNS	ADJECTIVES PARTICIPLES
	-ung	bedeutend - important
beissen - bite	(i)	(i) -ig
	die Biegung - bend,turn	-sam
brechen - break	(u)	(ü) -ig
		dauerhaft - lasting
	die Fahrt - drive, journey	-bar
fälschen - falsify	-ung	-lich
	-heit	gleich - equal
helfen - help	(i) -e	(i) -reich
	die Kürze - shortness	(u)
(au)	(au)	geläufig - fluent
lügen - lie	-ner	-nerisch
messen - measure	(a)	(ä) -ig
er-	-igkeit	müde - tired
-ern	die Nähe - nearness	(a) -e

öffnen - open	-nung	(o)
		ratsam - advisable
rauben - rob	(") -er	(") -erisch
-igen	-igung	rein - clean
schwächen - weaken	-e	(a)
	die Sorge - care	-sam
springen - jump	(u)	(u) -haft
	Ge-(ä)	trinkbar - drinkable
	die Vergesslichkeit- forgetfulness	-lich
zwingen - compel, force	(a)	-d

KEY TO PRACTICES

Practice 1 :

ride	deep	drive	deed	red	loud	devil
wade	fold	blood	need	card	dear	word
thorn	North	earth	feather	thinker	thistle	thirst
thunder	thin	three	thine			
tin	tell	greet	better	cat	toll	plant
twig	tongue	net	salt	heat	seat	twenty
pepper	post	penny	soap	weapon	sheep	up
leap	harp	bishop		ship	sleep	
strive	sieve	raven	weave	heave	even	have
break	speak	rake	wake	week	yoke	beaker
weight	fight	freight	light	thought	might	eight

Practice 2 :

1. The steward brings coffee, tea and cold cuts with bread, butter and cheese.
2. The thistles on the heath have sharp thorns. 3. The cat sits in the field;
it is hungry and wants a mouse. 4. They brought eight lights into the house
and were awake until midnight. 5. Maria has blond hair, blue eyes and a long
nose. 6. In the Alps in summer they can wander, fish, swim and sail. 7. Most
tourists go abroad and write postcards to their families. 8. The passenger
stares at the ocean water. What does he see in the water ? It is an iceberg.
9. If all goes well we will land in Frankfurt in ten minutes. 10. The cook
bakes apple cake and makes meat soup. 11. When it is cool he does not ride down
to the valley. 12. The old father has two sons and one daughter.

Practice 3 :

der Militarist	militaristisch
der Sozialist	sozialistisch
der Positivist	positivistisch
der Nihilist	nihilistisch
der Tourist	touristisch
der Separatist	separatistisch
der Realist	realistisch
der Nationalist	nationalistisch
der Marxist	marxistisch
der Humanist	humanistisch
der Anarchist	anarchistisch
der Darwinist	darwinistisch
der Opportunist	opportunistisch
der Optimist	optimistisch
der Pessimist	pessimistisch

Practice 4 :

der Rhetoriker	rhetorisch
der Physiker	physikalisch
der Methodiker	methodisch
der Analytiker	analytisch
der Graphiker	graphisch
der Metaphysiker	metaphysisch
der Pragmatiker	pragmatisch
der Botaniker	botanisch
der Statistiker	statistisch
der Techniker	technisch
der Politiker	politisch
der Klassiker	klassisch

Practice 5 :

der Diplomat	diplomatisch
der Biograph	biographisch
der Ökonom	ökonomisch
der Geograph	geographisch
der Fotograf	fotografisch
der Bürokrat	bürokratisch
der Philosoph	philosophisch
der Philologe	philologisch
der Theologe	theologisch
der Psychologe	psychologisch

Practice 6 :

demonstrieren
variieren
qualifizieren
konzentrieren
immigrieren
kolonisieren
reservieren
kombinieren
delegieren
deklamieren
klassifizieren
illuminieren
amputieren
produzieren
definieren
polarisieren
kulminieren

Practice 7 :
A.   1.b. - 2.a. - 3.d. - 4.e. - 5.c.
B.   1.a. - 2.e. - 3.c. - 4.d. - 5.b.
C.   1.e. - 2.b. - 3.d. - 4.c. - 5.a.
D.   1.b. - 2.d. - 3.e. - 4.c. - 5.a.

Practice 8 :

A.   1.d. - 2.e. - 3.c. - 4.a. - 5.b.

B.   1.d. - 2.b. - 3.c. - 4.e. - 5.a.

C.   1.c. - 2.d. - 3.e. - 4.a. - 5.b.

D.   1.b. - 2.a. - 3.d. - 4.e. - 5.c.

Practice 9 :
1. Mozartstrasse - 2. Nachttischlampe - 3. Mittagessen - 4. Schlafzimmermöbel
5. Kleiderbürste - 6. Telefonnummer - 7. Kinderheim - 8. Reissuppe
9. Blumengeschäft- 10. Stadtkirche

Practice 10 :

        die Verkehrsregelung
        das Gotteshaus
        der Jahresbericht
        die Lebenszeit
        das Waldesrauschen
        das Wohnungsfenster
        die Landesgrenze
        der Bundespräsident
        die Freundestreue
        der Volkswagen
        der Schiffskapitän
        der Betriebsleiter
        der Gutsherr
        der Gesichtsausdruck

Practice 11 :

        1.j. - 2.i. - 3.h. - 4.f. - 5.d. - 6.b. - 7.a. - 8.c. -
        9.g. - 10.k. - 11.e. - 12.1.

Practice 12 :

        der Blumentopf   -   die Topfblume
        das Ballspiel   -   der Spielball
        der Landesfeind   -   das Feindesland
        die Verkehrsstrasse   -   der Strassenverkehr
        der Baumstamm   -   der Stammbaum
        die Fleischsuppe   -   das Suppenfleisch
        der Höhenflug   -   die Flughöhe
        das Grenzgebiet   -   die Gebietsgrenze
        das Kleiderhaus   -   das Hauskleid
        die Tagesarbeit   -   der Arbeitstag

Practice 13 :

die Jungfrau	virgin
der Vollmond	full moon
die Kurzschrift	shorthand
die Rohseide	raw silk
der Dummkopf	blockhead
die Halbinsel	peninsula
das Doppelbett	double bed
die Hochschule	university
das Weissbrot	white bread
die Freizeit	leisure time
das Neujahr	New Year
der Rotwein	red wine
die Schwarzbeere	blackberry
der Gelbfilter	yellow filter
der Lautsprecher	loudspeaker
der Fernschreiber	teletype
der Frühsport	morning **drill**
der Edelmann	nobleman

Practice 15 :

A. 1.d. - 2.e. - 3. b. - 4.c. - 5.a.
B. 1.c. - 2.d. - 3. a. - 4.e. - 5.b.
C. 1.d. - 2.c. - 3. e. - 4.b. - 5.a.
D. 1.c. - 2.d. - 3. b. - 4.a. - 5.e.

Practice 16 :

der Rasierapparat	- razor	der Bindfaden	-	string
die Nähnadel	- sewing needle	der Kochtopf	-	cooking pot
der Parkplatz	- **parking lot**	die Laufbahn	-	career
die Waschmaschine	- washing machine	das Lehrbuch	-	textbook
das Trinkwasser	- drinking water	der Treibstoff	-	fuel
die Reitschule	- riding academy	die Lernfreiheit	-	freedom to learn
die Stehlampe	- floor-lamp	die Bratpfanne	-	frying pan
die Tankstelle	- service station	das Wohnhaus	-	residence

Practice 17 :

1. Kinderzimmer   2. Studierzimmer   3. Esszimmer   4. Arbeitszimmer
5. Schlafzimmer   6. Lesezimmer   7. Badezimmer   8. Rauchzimmer
9. Wartezimmer   10. Krankenzimmer

Practice 18 :

exit
emigrant
export
expression
outlook
departure

dessert
surname
afternoon
disadvantage
postlude
late summer
epilogue

hind foot
rear axle
background
rear wheel
back seat
rear view
back

Practice 19 :

ein Waldweg
ein Morgenstern
eine Bratpfanne
eine Eisenbahnfahrt
Rheinlieder
ein Abendessen
ein Parkplatz
eine Kellertreppe
die Nachtarbeit
eine Abendzeitung
ein Blindenhund
eine Glastür
der Kleiderhaken
die Metallsäge
eine Bärenstimme
das Feindesland
die Rohseide

Practice 20 :

1. Five-year plan   2. two-cycle engine   3. Feast of Epiphany   4. centennial
5. bus terminal   6. soccer championship   7. highway construction   8. streetcar
stop   9. unemployment compensation   10. four-color print   11. twelve-point
program   12. seven-months baby   13. subway   14. midnight hour   15. life
insurance company   16. highway regulations   17. space exploration   18. pollution

Practice 21 :

silberhell	(silverly)
kristallklar	(as clear as a crystal)
kinderleicht	(child's play)
turmhoch	(head and shoulders above)
steinhart	(as hard as stone)
riesengross	(gigantic)
bleischwer	**(heavy as lead)**
pechschwarz	(pitch black)
blitzschnell	(as quick as lightning)
messerscharf	(as sharp as a knife)

<u>Practice 22</u> :

A.   1.c. - 2.e. - 3.d. - 4.a. - 5.b.

B.   1.b. - 2.d. - 3.c. - 4.e. - 5.a.

C.   1.e. - 2.d. - 3.b. - 4.c. - 5.a.

<u>Practice 23</u> :

    1.j. - 2.g. - 3.b. - 4.f. - 5.i. - 6.c. - 7.e. - 8.d. -
    9.h. - 10.a.

<u>Practice 24</u> :

1. friedliebend   2. silberglänzend   3. notleidend   4. grundlegend   5. welt-
umspannend   6. diensthabend   7. aufsehenerregend   8. gesundheitsschädigend
9. postlagernd   10. gefahrdrohend

<u>Practice 25</u> :

1. a face red with anger   2. a bomb-damaged city   3. a sun-drenched landscape
4. a war-disabled man   5. a wood-carved altar   6. a gold-decorated book
7. a remote-controlled plane   8. a passionately loved girl

<u>Practice 26</u> :

    1.k. - 2.j. - 3.b. - 4.1. - 5.i. - 6.d. - 7.f. - 8.g. -
    9.a. - 10.c. - 11.e. - 12.h.

<u>Practice 27</u> :

A.   1. pay out   2. unhinge   3. disembark   4. unpack   5. get out   6. breathe
      out   7. turn off 8. remove   9. pour out 10.unload   11. exhume
    12. march out

B.   1. draw   2. lock   3. button   4. turn off 5.roll up   6. close
      7. close   8. buckle   9. lace up   10. screw on 11.tie up

C.   1. switch off   2. turn off   3. cancel   4. take off   5. give notice of
      leaving   6. give up   7. take off   8. extinguish   9. jump off   10. go
      off the stage   11. unload   12. dismount   13. lose weight   14. cancel,
      call off   15. flow off   16. underexpose   17. underbid   18. underestimate
      19. inferior   20. follow   21. set back   22. follow

<u>Practice 28</u> :

1. Please turn off the engine.   2. Did you turn in your exam already ?
3. I delivered the letter to his address.   4. I lost a button.   5. He likes
to push the others aside.   6. The teacher calls the student aside.

7. I am putting away the money for my old age.   8. The car drove off with dimmed lights. 9. We managed to get away once more. 10. The thief made off hastily. 11. The child ran away from his parents. 12. I will not let you go away so soon. 13. I hope we will get away from here in time. 14. The troops will pull out tomorrow. 15. He took the car keys away from me. 16. The children put away the toys and helped their mother. 17. She looked away when she saw him. 18. The train left a few minutes ago. 19. The ship broke loose from its anchor. 20. He got into the car and drove away.

Practice 29 :

       1.j. - 2.b. - 3.1. - 4.c. - 5.k. - 6.d. - 7.h. - 8.m. -
       9.e. - 10.g. - 11.f. - 12.i. - 13.a.

Practice 30 :

       1.c. - 2.f. - 3.g. - 4.1. - 5.m. - 6.e. - 7.b. - 8.r. -
       9.h. - 10.k. - 11.n. - 12.q. - 13.a. - 14.d. - 15.i. - 16.j. -
       17.o. - 18.p.

Practice 31 :

A.   1. arrive   2. call (up) 3. accept   4. listen to 5. tie up 6. cling to
      7. screw on   8. address   9. grow on 10. touch

B.   1. start   2. start a fire 3. gnaw   4. start to saw, cut   5. to brown
      6. train   7. make the first cut   8. start   9. break open
   10. start

C.   1. lock up   2. wear out   3. cut off   4. break off   5. eat up completely
      6. work off (clear off)   7. fatten   8. refill (fill up)   9. pump up
   10. turn up, stir   11. empty, drain   12. pour out   13. eat up   14. serve
   one's time   15. finish learning

Practice 32 :

       1.c. - 2.d. - 3.j. - 4.f. - 5.e. - 6.i. - 7.h. - 8.g. -
       9.a. - 10.b.

Practice 33 :

1. No singing or noise making.   2. Do not cross the tracks.   3. No passing on curves.   4. No smoking.   5. Keep off the lawn.   6. Do not open the windows. 7. Do not talk to the driver.   8. No swimming and bathing in this river. 9. Do not lean bicycles against the wall (building).   10. Do not eat food you brought along.

Practice 34 :

1. Mass   2. Zug   3. Flucht   4. Flug   5. Sprung   6. Zwang   7. Bruch
8. Schuss 9. Schluss   10. Bund   11. Schwund   12. Gang   13. Griff   14. -wuchs

Practice 35 :

1. der Ärger	(anger)	11. der Rat	(advice)
2. der Bann	(ban)	12. der Schrei	(scream)
3. der Dank	(gratitude,thanks)	13. der Scherz	(joke)
4. die Feier	(celebration)	14. der Schlag	(blow, stroke)
5. der Handel	(trade)	15. der Spalt	(split, cleft)
6. die Heirat	(marriage)	16. der Spott	(mockery)
7. das Kleid	(dress)	17. der Sitz	(seat)
8. der Kampf	(fight)	18. der Teil	(part)
9. der Lauf	(run, course)	19. das Wunder	(miracle, wonder)
10.das Lob	(praise)	20. die Wut	(rage)

Practice 36 :

1. Fang   2. Wahl   3. Schwur   4. Gewinn   5. Bau   6. Fluss   7. Kauf
8. Besitz

Practice 37 :

1.l. - 2.m. - 3.j. - 4.h. - 5.f. - 6.g. - 7.d. - 8.e. -
9.b. - 10.c. - 11.k. - 12.i. - 13.a.

Practice 38 :

1.d. - 2.t. - 3.m. - 4.l. - 5.n. - 6.q. - 7.a. - 8.k. -
9.o. - 10.p. - 11.s. - 12.r. - 13.e. - 14.f. - 15.g. - 16.j. -
17.h. - 18.i. - 19.c. - 20.b.

Practice 39 :

die Bitte	(request)
die Frage	(question)
der Glaube	(faith)
die Lehre	(teaching)
die Lüge	(lie)
die Pflege	(care)
die Aussage	(statement)
die Anklage	(accusation)
die Auslese	(selection)
die Nachfrage	(inquiry)

Practice 40 :

1. die Kürze des Lebens   2. die Schwere der Arbeit   3. die Stille der Natur
4. die Süsse des Honigs   5. die Härte des Stahls   6. die Röte des Himmels
7. die Länge des Stromes   8. die Milde des Klimas   9. die Kälte des Winters
10.die Enge des Pfades

Practice 41 :

1. working   work   worker   (female) worker
2. visiting   visit   visitor   (female) visitor
3. serving   service   servant   (female) servant
4. cooking   cook   cooker   (female) cook
5. teaching   teaching   teacher   (female) teacher
6. smoking   smoke   smoker   (female) smoker
7. cutting   cut   tailor   dressmaker
8. dancing   dance   dancer   (female)dancer
9. selling   sale   salesman   saleslady
10.voting   election   voter

Practice 42 :

1. Radfahrer   2. Skiläufer   3. Nichtstuer   4. Nichtraucher   5. Kleidermacher
6. Buchdrucker   7. Uhrmacher   8. Fensterputzer   9. Landschaftsmaler
10. Ehebrecher   11. Langschläfer   12. Arbeitgeber

Practice 43 :

1. Zeichnen   2. Fliegen   3. Lesen   4. Schwimmen   5. Segeln   6. Rudern
7. Singen   8. Laufen   9. Reiten 10. Jagen

Practice 44 :

1. Rohköstler   2. Erzgebirgler   3. Wissenschaftler   4. Sommerfrischler
5. Zuchthäusler 6. Arbeitsrechtler

1. Gärtner   2. Glöckner   3. Harfner   4. Bühnenbildner
5. Lügner

1. Täufling   2. Findling   3. Nachkömmling   4. Zögling
5. Pflegling   6. Frechling

Practice 45 :

1. Brauerei   2. Druckerei   3. Fleischerei   4. Försterei   5. Gärtnerei
6. Schlosserei   7. Schneiderei   8. Schreinerei   9. Spinnerei   10. Weberei

<u>Practice 46</u> :

1. gluttony   2. cringing   3. indiscriminate reading   4. small talk
5. big talk, boasting   6. brawl, fight   7. aimless shooting   8. magic, sorcery

<u>Practice 47</u> :

a.)   1. die Schönheit der Frau
      2. die Krankheit des Kindes
      3. die Dunkelheit der Nacht
      4. die Frechheit des Jungen
      5. die Echtheit des Diamanten
      6. die Beliebtheit des Dichters
      7. die Gewissheit des Todes
      8. die Trockenheit des Sommers
      9. die Klugheit des Tieres
     10. die Wahrheit der Geschichte

b.)   1. die Gefährlichkeit des Verkehrs
      2. die Ewigkeit Gottes
      3. die Veränderlichkeit des Wetters
      4. die Tapferkeit des Soldaten
      5. die Vergesslichkeit des Professors
      6. die Heiligkeit des Tempels
      7. die Sauberkeit der Wohnung
      8. die Wichtigkeit der Forschung
      9. die Tüchtigkeit der Sekretärin
     10. die Höflichkeit der Bewohner

<u>Practice 48</u> :

              1. Hemmnis   (obstruction)
              2. Hindernis   (hindrance)
              3. Ereignis   (occurrence)
              4. Ergebnis   (result)
              5. Erlebnis   (experience)
              6. Erzeugnis   (product)
              7. Gelübnis   (vow)
              8. Geständnis   (confession)
              9. Vermächtnis   (bequest)
             10. Versäumnis   (omission)

<u>Practice 49</u> :

1. die Bürgerschaft   2. die Dienerschaft   3. die Bauernschaft   4. die
Kollegenschaft   5. die Mitgliedschaft   6. die Nachbarschaft   7. die Lehrer-
schaft   8. die Studentenschaft   9. die Nachkommenschaft   10. die Priester-
schaft

Practice 50 :

1.	die Bedeutung	(meaning)
2.	die Handlung	(act, deed)
3.	die Erziehung	(education)
4.	die Regierung	(government)
5.	die Erfahrung	(experience)
6.	die Reinigung	(cleaning)
7.	die Vorlesung	(lecture)
8.	die Beschäftigung	**(employment)**
9.	die Rettung	(rescue)
10.	die Verbindung	(connection)
11.	die Übung	(exercise, practice)
12.	die Achtung	(respect)

Practice 51 :

1. Edison erfand das Grammophon.   2. Columbus entdeckte Amerika.   3. Der Regen erfrischte uns angenehm.   4. Die Wunde heilte nur sehr langsam.   5. Er unterhielt die Gäste mit Radiomusik.   6. Die Tiere dürfen nicht gefüttert werden.   7. Kleiden Sie sich warm, sonst werden Sie sich erkälten.   8. Die Kinder zu erziehen ist heutzutage sehr schwer.   9. Die beiden Männer begegneten sich gestern.   10. Wir müssen uns entscheiden.

Practice 52 :

das Gefieder	(feathers)
das Gehölz	(thicket of small trees)
das Gemäuer	(masonwork)
das Geflügel	(poultry)
das Gericht	(court)
das Gesträuch	(shrubs)
das Gebrüll	(roaring)
das Gefolge	(retinue)
das Gefühl	(sentiment)
der Geruch	(smell)
das Geschenk	(gift)
das Gepäck	(luggage)
das Gewächs	(growth)

Practice 53 :

spoils, prey	shrubbery
epic poetry	foliage
spiritual values	masonry, brickwork
knowledge	**rigging**
educational system	lighter
railway system	writing implements
film industry	footwear
Public Health	school things

Practice 54 :

1.	Sie ist lösbar.	(soluble)
2.	Sie ist befahrbar.	(negotiable)
3.	Er ist sichtbar.	(visible)
4.	Es ist bewohnbar.	(habitable)
5.	Sie ist brauchbar.	(useable)
6.	Er ist hörbar.	(audible)
7.	Es ist trinkbar.	(drinkable)
8.	Sie ist teilbar.	(divisible)
9.	Es ist waschbar.	(washable)
10.	Es ist nicht definierbar.	(undefinable)
11.	Er ist tragbar.	(portable)
12.	Er ist gangbar.	(practicable, negotiable)

Practice 55 :

1.	eine Tür aus Glas	eine Glastür
2.	ein Tuch aus Wolle	ein Wolltuch
3.	ein Löffel aus Silber	ein Silberlöffel
4.	ein Hut aus Samt	ein Samthut
5.	ein Gitter aus Eisen	ein Eisengitter
6.	ein Kessel aus Kupfer	ein Kupferkessel
7.	ein Tischtuch aus Papier	ein Papiertischtuch
8.	ein Tisch aus Eiche	ein Eichentisch

Practice 56 :

1.	dauerhaft	(lasting)
2.	vorteilhaft	(profitable)
3.	schmerzhaft	(painful)
4.	schadhaft	(defective, faulty)
5.	traumhaft	(dreamy)
6.	naschhaft	(fond of dainties)
7.	schwatzhaft	(talkative)
8.	schamhaft	(bashful)
9.	lasterhaft	(vicious, immoral)
10.	glaubhaft	(credible)

Practice 57 :

1. Er ist eifrig und ehrgeizig.   2. Er ist begierig zu lernen.   3. Wir sind hungrig und durstig.   4. Süddeutschland ist waldig und gebirgig.   5. Ihr Gesicht ist faltig.   6. Die Suppe ist zu salzig und pfefferig.   7. Er ist schuldig an diesem Unglück.   8. Seien Sie gütig und nehmen Sie das zurück. 9. Die hiesige Bevölkerung interessiert sich nicht dafür.   10. Die heutige Jugend lebt anders als die gestrige.   11. Bitte kommen Sie rechtzeitig. 12. Das Brot ist schwammig.   13. Die alten Freunde sassen einträchtig bei- sammen.   14. Wir haben alles geduldig und ruhig ertragen.   15. Der Wein schmeckt wässerig.   16. Er trägt einen breitrandigen Hut.   17. Dachshunde sind kurzbeinig.   18. Das Flugzeug ist zweimotorig.

Practice 58 :

heldisch	(heroic)	höhnisch	(scornful)
herrisch	(imperious)	magisch	(magic)
jüdisch	(Jewish)	paradiesisch	(heavenly)
mörderisch	(murderous)	parteiisch	(partial)
schöpferisch	(creative)	rassisch	(racial)
studentisch	(studentlike)	schulisch	(pertaining to schools)
verschwenderisch	(lavish)	stürmisch	(stormy)
weibisch	(womanish)	tropisch	(tropical)

Practice 59 :

1. Westfalen
2. Frankreich
3. England
4. Irland
5. Norwegen

6. Rheinland
7. Preussen
8. Spanien
9. Russland
10. Finnland

Practice 60 :

1. täglich   2. wöchentlich   3. stündlich   4. nächtliche   5. zerbrechlich
6. geschäftlich   7. kränklich   8. süssliche   9. augenblicklich
10. königliche   11. sprachlichen   12. inhaltlich   13. künstliche
14. verkäuflich   15. zeitlichen

Practice 61 :

1. to write poetry - poet - poem - poetry - work of poetry - poetic
2. to invent - inventor - invention - inventiveness - inventive
3. to eat - eating, meal - eater - (indiscriminate) eating - edible - edibility
4. to ask - question - questioner (inquirer) - incessant questioning - questionable - questionableness
5. to live, dwell - house - domestic - family life - as high as a house, very high
6. to buy - purchase - buyer - purchasable - merchant - commercial
7. to land - land - landing - rural - landscape - terrain, tract of land
8. to paint - painter - female painter - painting - picturesque - the painting
9. to dream - dream - dreamer - dreamy - dreamy - reverie
10. to live - apartment - residing - livable - livability - residence

Practice 62 :

ein friedsamer Mensch
ein sittsamer Mensch
ein ehrsamer Mensch
ein sorgsamer Mensch
ein enthaltsamer Mensch
ein fügsamer Mensch
eine mühsame Arbeit
ein erholsamer Urlaub
ein gewaltsamer Tod

Practice 63 :

1. expressionless   2. safe, without risk   3. unfeeling, insensible
4. noiseless   5. powerless   6. inconsiderate   7. worthless   8. not spicy
9. helpless   10. childless   11. waterless, dry   12. faultless   13. dust-free
14. useless

Practice 64 :

1.i. - 2.d. - 3.j. - 4.a. - 5.l. - 6.b. - 7.c. - 8.f. -
9.g. - 10.e. - 11.h. - 12.k.

Practice 65 :

andernfalls	(otherwise)
gleichfalls	(likewise)
schlimmstenfalls	(at worst)
besonders	(especially)
links	(left)
rechts	(right)
weiters	(furthermore)
mittels	(by means of)
nachmittags	(in the afternoon)
winters	(in winter)
zwecks	(for the purpose of)
bestens	(best)
mindestens	(at least)
längstens	(at the latest)
schnellstens	(in the fastest possible way)
dummerweise	(foolishly)
unglucklicherweise	(unfortunately)
leihweise	(on loan)
gruppenweise	(in groups)
massenweise	(in masses)
versuchsweise	(experimentally)

Practice 66 :

nachtmahlen	geigen
krönen	lüften
grasen	färben
ochsen	besohlen
anketten	feilen
gondeln	klecksen

Practice 67 :

ändern
bräunen
glätten
krümmen

lockern
schärfen
dunkeln
heilen
kühlen
nässen

Practice 68 :

1. schwänzeln
2. schlängeln
3. häufeln
4. betteln
5. witzeln
6. zerstückeln
7. kriseln
8. fälteln
9. krabbeln
10. näseln

Practice 69 :

abstract
add
amuse oneself
anglicize
decorate
demolish
denounce
depress
discuss
experiment

force
formulate
function
harmonize
command
compose
correct
critisize
march
note

number
operate
polish
try, probe
protest
rationalize
respect
simplify
synchronize
wire, telegraph

Practice 70 :

die Unaufmerksamkeit	(inattention)
die Unbequemlichkeit	(inconvenience)
der Unfriede	(discord)
der Ungehorsam	(disobedience)
die Ungleichheit	(inequality)
das Unglück	(misfortune, bad luck)
die Ungunst	(disfavor)
das Unrecht	(injustice)
der Unsegen	(curse, adversity)
die Unsitte	(bad habit)
die Untreue	(disloyalty)
die Untugend	(vice, bad habit)
das Unvermögen	(inability, incapacity)
die Unvernunft	(unreasonableness, lack of reason)
die Unwahrheit	(untruth)
die Unzufriedenheit	(dissatisfaction)

Practice 71 :

    1. ein unbekannter Dichter
    2. ein unverheiratetes Mädchen
    3. ungebildete Menschen
    4. ein ungeordnetes Leben
    5. unverstandene Jugend
    6. ungewaschene Hände
    7. ungelesene Bücher
    8. ungestempelte Briefmarken
    9. ungeschliffene Edelsteine
  10. ungeschützte Grenzen

Practice 72 :

A.   1. unzerstörbar
     2. unzählbar
     3. unsagbar
     4. unberechenbar
     5. unschätzbar
     6. untrennbar
     7. undenkbar
     8. untragbar
     9. unlösbar
   10. unheilbar

B.   1. unbeweglich
     2. unabänderlich
     3. unzerbrechlich
     4. unaussprechlich
     5. unglaublich
     6. unbeschreiblich
     7. unleserlich
     8. unbegreiflich
     9. unausstehlich
   10. unentbehrlich

Practice 73 :

    1. Die Fremden bestaunten die Schönheit des Landes.
    2. Sie beklagten den Verlust.
    3. Kannst du mich beraten ?
    4. Wie beurteilen Sie die politische Lage ?
    5. Die Firma beliefert nur ausländische Kunden.
    6. Ein mächtiger König beherrschte das Land.
    7. Es ist eine sportliche Leistung,diesen Berg zu besteigen.
    8. Wer bezahlt die Getränke ?
    9. Das Heer bekämpfte einen mächtigen Feind.
  10. Können Sie die Theaterkarten besorgen ?

Practice 74 :

 1. Wann können Sie die Arbeit beenden ?
 2. Es ist nicht zu bestreiten, dass Sie recht haben.
 3. Warum bezweifeln Sie meine Erklärungen ?
 4. Der Tote wurde gestern begraben.
 5. Die Soldaten bestürmten die feindlichen Stellungen.
 6. Sie haben den Film zu lange belichtet.
 7. Jedes Blatt muss deutlich beschriftet werden.
 8. Sie sollen sich Ihr Auto neu bereifen lassen.
 9. Darf ich Sie zu Ihrer Beförderung beglückwünschen.
10. Wir haben uns kürzlich mit dieser Familie befreundet.

Practice 75 :

1. entkräften 2. entwaffnen 3. entsalzen 4. entblättern 5. entwerten
6. enthaupten 7. entkorken 8. entkernen 9. entlasten 10. entwässern
11.entwurzeln 12.enthärten

Practice 76 :

1. Das Bad hat mich wieder erfrischt. 2. Er hat mir das ermöglicht. 3. Der
lange Marsch hat ihn ermüdet. 4. Du erschwerst mir die Arbeit. 5. Moderne
Erfindungen erleichtern uns das Leben. 6. Gib acht, dass du nicht erkrankst.
7. Sie errötete bis über die Ohren. 8. Sein Haar begann zu ergrauen. 9. Meine
Finger sind ganz erstarrt. 10. Die Kinder ermüden schnell.

Practice 77 :

1. Wir erbitten Ihre Hilfe. 2. Ich habe mir das Geld für ein Auto erspart.
3. Die Soldaten erstürmten die Burg. 4. Er erschlug ihn. 5. Wir mussten den
Hund erschiessen. 6. Er ergriff ihre Hand. 7. Wir erhoffen alle bessere
Zeiten. 8. Sie haben ein Wiedersehen mit uns ersehnt. 9. Er erarbeitete
ein eigenes Häuschen. 10. Du hast den besten Teil erwählt. 11. Ich erwarte
dich um 10 Uhr in der Bibliothek. 12. Der Arzt erforschte die Ursachen der
Krankheit.

Practice 78 :

verdeutlichen	(make plain)
vervollkommnen	(improve, perfect)
vereinfachen	(simplify)
verdicken	(thicken)
verstaatlichen	(nationalize)
versüssen	(sweeten)
verwässern	(water down)
vergrössern	(enlarge)
verbreitern	(widen)
verbessern	(improve)
verschönern	(beautify)

verkürzen	(shorten)
vertiefen	(deepen)
verstärken	(amplify)

Practice 79 :

versalzen	put too much salt in
sich verhören	hear wrong
verstecken	hide
den Kopf verdrehen	turn one's head
verkennen	fail to realize
verschreiben	make a slip of the pen
den Fuss vertreten	sprain one's ankle
verstimmt	out of tune
verwöhnen	spoil
sich verlaufen	lose one's way
verkehrt	upside down
sich verlesen	misread
sich verschlafen	oversleep
Geld vertun	waste money
verwechseln	mix up

Practice 80 :

Die Blätter verwelken schon.	(dry up)
Das Holz verfault.	(rot, decay)
Die Musik verklingt.	(die away)
Das Tier verdurstet.	(die of thirst)
Das Feuer verglüht im Ofen.	(die away)
Das Brot verschimmelt.	(get moldy)
Die alten Häuser verfallen.	(crumble, dilapidate)
Das Kind verblutet.	(bleed to death)
Das Echo verhallt.	(die away)

Practice 81 :

1. take apart   2. chop up   3. analyze   4. cut to pieces, slice   5. tear up
6. smash   7. pluck to pieces   8. saw up   9. cook to rags   10. disperse
11.trample underfoot   12. crush

Practice 82 :

| misshandeln | (ill-treat) |
| die Misshandlung | (ill-treatment) |

| missbilden | (misshape) |
| die Missbildung | (deformity) |

missbilligen	(disapprove)
die Missbilligung	(disapproval)
missbrauchen	(to misuse, abuse)
der Missbrauch	(the misuse, abuse)
missfallen	(displease)
das Missfallen	(displeasure, dislike)
missgönnen	(to envy, grudge)
die Missgunst	(envy)
misstrauen	(to distrust)
das Misstrauen	(the distrust)
missverstehen	(misunderstand)
das Missverständnis	(misunderstanding)
missvergnügt	(displeased, malcontent)
das Missvergnügen	(displeasure)

Practice 83 :

A.   1.d. - 2.a. - 3.b. - 4.c. - 5.e.

B.   1.c. - 2.d. - 3.b. - 4.e. - 5.a.

C.   1.e. - 2.a. - 3.b. - 4.d. - 5.c.

D.   1.a. - 2.c. - 3.b. - 4.e. - 5.d.

E.   1.e. - 2.d. - 3.c. - 4.a. - 5.b.

F.   1.e. - 2.c. - 3.a. - 4.d. - 5.b.

VERBS		NOUNS		ADJECTIVES (PARTICIPLES)	
bedeuten	- mean	die Bedeutung	- meaning	bedeutend	- important
beissen	- bite	der Biss	- bite	bissig	- snappish
biegen	- bend	die Biegung	- bend, turn	biegsam	- flexible
brechen	- break	der Bruch	- breach	brüchig	- fragile
dauern	- last	die Dauer	- duration	dauerhaft	- lasting
fahren	- go, drive	die Fahrt	- drive, journey	fahrbar	- movable
fälschen	- falsify	die Fälschung	- falsification	fälschlich	- false
gleichen	- equal	die Gleichheit	- equality	gleich	- equal
helfen	- help	die Hilfe	- help	hilfreich	- helpful
kürzen	- shorten	die Kürze	- shortness	kurz	- short
laufen	- run, flow	der Lauf	- run, course	geläufig	- fluent
lügen	- lie	der Lügner	- liar	lügnerisch	- lying, false
messen	- measure	das Mass	- measure	mässig	- moderate
ermüden	- tire	die Müdigkeit	- fatigue	müde	- tired
nähern	- approach	die Nähe	- nearness	nahe	- near
öffnen	- open	die Öffnung	- opening	offen	- open
raten	- advise	der Rat	- advice	ratsam	- advisable
rauben	- rob	der Räuber	- robber	räuberisch	- rapacious
reinigen	- clean	die Reinigung	- cleaning	rein	- clean
schwächen	- weaken	die Schwäche	- weakness	schwach	- weak
sorgen	- care	die Sorge	- care	sorgsam	- careful
springen	- jump	der Sprung	- jump	sprunghaft	- jerky
trinken	- drink	das Getränk	- drink	trinkbar	- drinkable
vergessen	- forget	die Vergesslichkeit	- forgetfulness	vergesslich	- forgetful
zwingen	- compel, force	der Zwang	- compulsion	zwingend	- imperative

The End